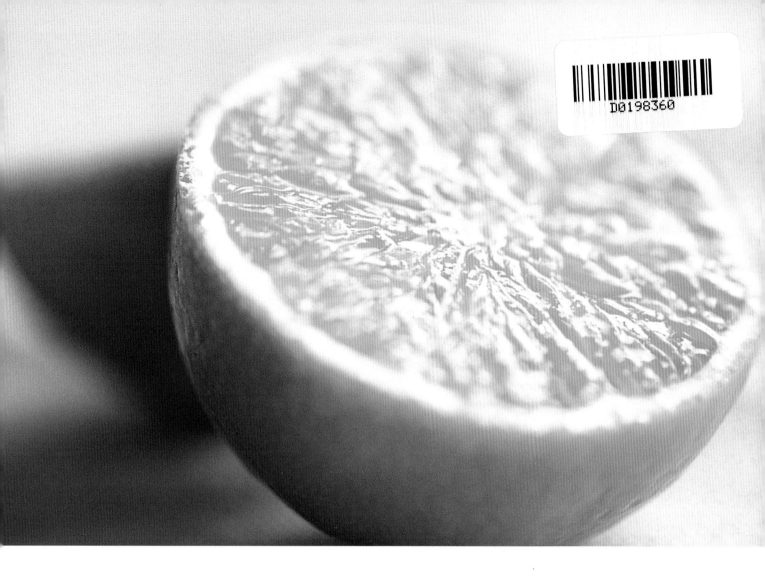

simple food

text and photographs
by Jill Dupleix

Quadrille

simple food

Jill Dupleix

NOTES
All spoon measures are level;
1 tsp=5 ml spoon, 1 tbsp=15 ml spoon.
All recipe ideas serve 4 unless
otherwise suggested. All eggs are
free-range and large; all herbs are
fresh; all salt is sea salt, and all
pepper is freshly ground black pepper
unless otherwise stated.

Creative Director Mary Evans
with design assistance from
Rachel Gibson and Katy Davis
Project Editor Janet Illsley
Production Nancy Roberts

First published in 2002 by
Quadrille Publishing Limited
Alhambra House
27-31 Charing Cross Road
London WC2H OLS

This paperback edition first published
in 2003

Cataloguing in Publication Data: a
catalogue record for this book is
available from the British Library.

ISBN 1 84400 016 8
Printed in Singapore

contents

Manifesto

I call this simple food for complicated people.

It's all about how to get home tonight, have a glass of wine, and be eating something delicious – fast roast fish, little ham and egg pies, or parmesan lamb cutlets – within half an hour. It's also about slow food that cooks itself, such as figs and baked ricotta, or baked potato with blue cheese. And food that's almost patronisingly easy, as in the world's simplest recipe for creamy banana ice-cream.

I love to cook, but I don't want to be cooking when I could be eating and drinking. My food philosophy – indeed, my entire philosophy – is to get away with doing as little as possible, as often as possible, by keeping things simple.

If you have great ingredients at their best, you can get away with doing less to them. There is no need for artificiality, because the real thing is good enough.

With Simple Food, techniques are everyday, tools are basic, and flavours are real. It's a way of getting the food part of your life under control, so that it does what it's meant to do – makes you feel good.

Simple, really.

simple starters

Sweetcorn shot soup

You won't believe how sweet this is. The trick is making the base stock with the stripped corn cobs, then adding the corn kernels for more flavour. Serve as a first course, or pour into shot glasses and serve as a chic appetizer with drinks.

Peel the outer leaves from the corn cobs, and discard the leaves and those pesky fine strings. Using a sharp knife, shear off the kernels and set aside. Place the corn cobs in a pan, cover with the cold water, add salt and simmer for 30 minutes, then strain, reserving the broth.

Finely chop the onion. Melt the butter in a pan, and cook the onion for 5 minutes. Add the corn kernels and the strained stock and simmer for 15 minutes. Whiz the soup in a blender until smooth, then strain through a fine sieve, pressing the juices through with a wooden spoon.

To serve, gently reheat the soup, whisk in the cream, salt, pepper and nutmeg, and simmer for 2 minutes. Serve hot, warm or chilled. This quantity will fill 4 soup bowls or 10 small shot glasses.

SERVES 4

4 corn cobs

1.5 litres cold water

sea salt

1 onion, peeled

1 tbsp butter

1 tbsp cream

freshly ground black pepper

1/4 tsp ground nutmeg

Tuna and white bean toast

Whiz 400 g drained, canned white beans and 200 g canned tuna with its oil in a blender. Add 2 anchovy fillets, black pepper and lemon juice and whiz again. Serve on grilled sourdough bread smeared with garlicky olive oil, with black olives and thyme on top.

Chipolata oysters

Cold oysters are great on their own, but they are even better with hot little sausages on the side. Take a bite of a hot, peppery beef chipolata, then slurp down a cold, salty, tangy oyster. Repeat until nothing is left.

Scrub the oysters well. Wrap a good thick tea towel around your left hand and hold an oyster firmly in your palm, the flat side facing upwards, the thin, pointy end towards you. Push the point of the knife firmly through the hinge, feeling your way, twisting the blade slightly and increasing the pressure until you feel it give way.

Wipe the blade free of any grit, and run it neatly under the top shell. Lift off the top shell, but keep the oyster steady so you don't lose its natural juices. Loosen the oyster from its shell and set the shell down on a bed of watercress or parsley. Repeat to open the rest of the oysters.

Lightly oil a non-stick fry pan. Prick the sausages well and pan-fry them gently, turning once or twice. When they are sizzling hot and cooked through, drain them on paper towel and arrange next to the oysters. Add the lime or lemon quarters and serve, with flutes of Champagne or tankards of beer.

SERVES 4
12 large fresh oysters
watercress or parsley sprigs
16 beef chipolata sausages
1 lime or lemon, quartered

Anchoiade toasts

Provençal anchovy paste has a strong and sunny flavour that makes it the perfect appetizer to have on toasted baguette with drinks in the sunshine. It is also delicious on hard-boiled eggs, or drizzled over roasted vegetables.

Using a pestle and mortar, pound the anchovies, tomato purée and garlic until smooth. Add the olive oil, drop by drop to begin with as you continue to pound, until you have a thick paste. Then add the oil by the teaspoonful, until the mixture is smooth and glossy. Beat in the orange juice and some pepper.

Finely slice the baguette into 20 or so slices, and grill on both sides until dry and golden. (You can do all this in advance.) Spoon a little anchoiade onto each toast to serve.

SERVES 6 TO 8

24 canned anchovy fillets
   in oil (2 small cans), drained
2 tbsp tomato purée (paste)
2 garlic cloves, peeled
4–5 tbsp extra virgin olive oil
1 tbsp orange juice
freshly ground black pepper
1 baguette

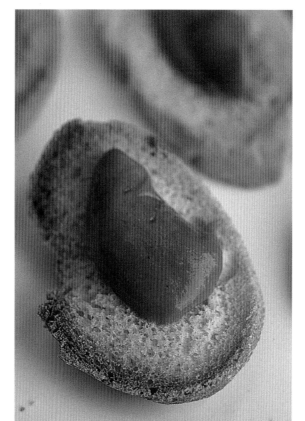

Spiced quail eggs

Boil 12 quail eggs in simmering water for 3 minutes. Cool in cold water, then peel and trim a slice off one end so they sit up. Dip the pointy end in smoked paprika and top with a flake of sea salt. Serve with drinks.

Tomato and basil bruschetta

Summer cooking is simple. Get up in the morning, do this to a few ripe tomatoes, leave them to infuse and go back to bed. The first course is almost done.

Cut out the cores from the tomatoes and cut a small cross at the base. Dunk them in a pot of boiling water for 20 seconds, then peel off the skins. Cut the tomatoes in half, squeeze out and discard the seeds and juice, and roughly chop the flesh.

Lightly toss the tomatoes in a bowl with the garlic cloves, basil leaves, sea salt, pepper and olive oil. Cover and set aside in a cool place to infuse. Do this an hour or two before you intend to eat.

When ready to serve, grill or toast the bread on both sides. Dip a pastry brush in the tomato marinade and brush each toast. Pile the tomatoes and basil on top, drizzle with the juices, and serve.

SERVES 4

4 ripe, red tomatoes

2 garlic cloves, peeled and
  smashed

1 cup basil leaves

sea salt

freshly ground black pepper

4 tbsp extra virgin olive oil

4 thick slices sourdough bread

Crumbed goat cheese salad

Buy cooked beetroot or, better still, cook your own beforehand, then team with flash-fried crumbed goat cheese for a fast and simple sit-down first course.

Cut the goat cheese into 4 slices, around 1 cm thick. Coat each slice in olive oil, then in the breadcrumbs, and chill until required.

Peel the cooked beetroot by rubbing off the skin. Trim neatly, slice into paper-thin rounds and arrange in an overlapping ring on each dinner plate. Whisk the dressing ingredients together in a bowl. Toss the rocket or spinach leaves lightly in the dressing and arrange in the centre of the beetroot.

Heat a non-stick fry pan, and dry-fry each slice of goat cheese until golden brown, carefully turning once. Gently lift the goat cheese onto the leaves (it may break up, but that's okay). Drizzle any remaining dressing over and around.

SERVES 4

200 g fresh, firm goat cheese
(in a round or log form)
2 tbsp extra virgin olive oil
3 tbsp fine, dry breadcrumbs
4 medium beetroot, cooked
200 g baby rocket or
spinach leaves

Dressing:
2 tbsp extra virgin olive oil
1 tbsp white wine vinegar
1 tbsp finely snipped chives
sea salt
freshly ground black pepper

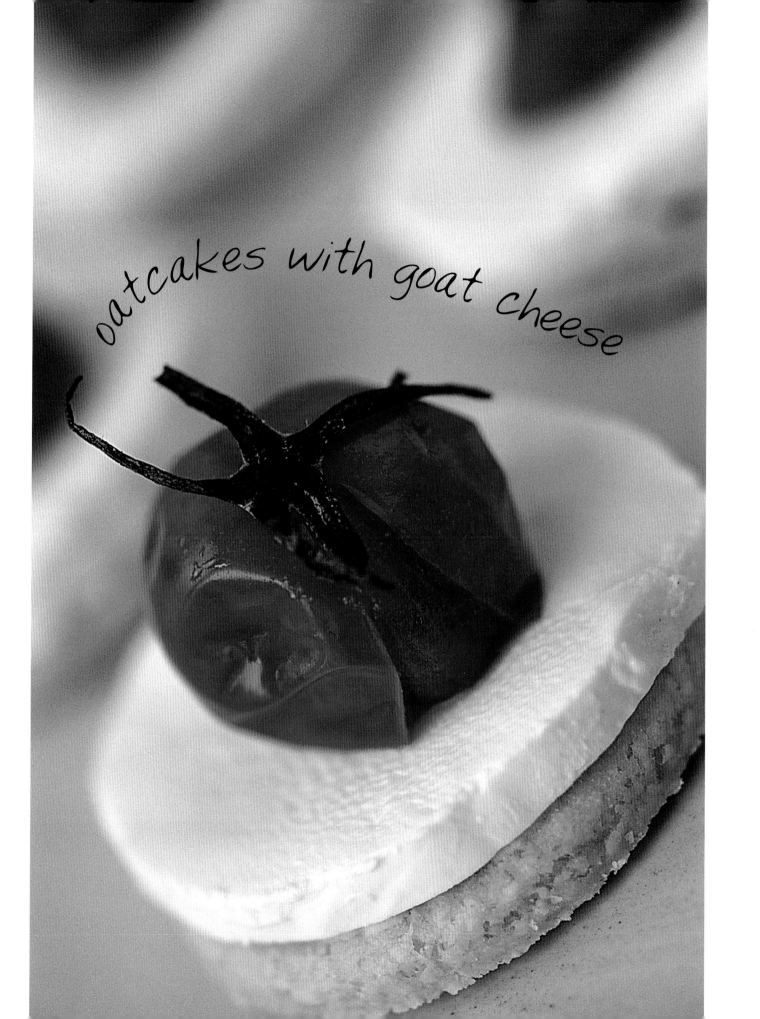

oatcakes with goat cheese

Gazpacho with cucumber

This isn't so much a cold soup, as a fresh and healthy vegetable smoothie. If you're feeling flash, drop a cooked prawn into each bowl, as a surprise bonus.

Roughly chop the tomatoes, cucumber, peppers, onion and garlic, and combine in a blender.

Cut off the crusts from the bread and discard. Place the bread in a bowl with just enough water to cover, then immediately squeeze out the water and roughly tear the bread into pieces.

Add the bread to the blender with the sherry vinegar, olive oil, Tabasco, sea salt and pepper. Whiz for a minute or two, until smooth. Press through a fine sieve into a bowl, then cover and chill until ready to serve.

Place a prawn (if using) in each chilled cocktail glass or serving bowl, and top with the vegetable gazpacho. Scatter diced sweet pepper and cucumber on top.

SERVES 4

6 ripe tomatoes

1 cucumber, peeled and seeded

2 sweet red peppers, cored
   and seeded

1 small onion, peeled

1 garlic clove, peeled

3 thick slices sourdough bread

2 tbsp sherry vinegar

2 tbsp extra virgin olive oil

dash of Tabasco

sea salt

freshly ground black pepper

To serve:

4 cooked prawns (optional)

2 tbsp diced sweet red pepper

2 tbsp diced cucumber

Oatcakes with goat cheese

Why make them when you can buy them? Because they're so much better homemade. Top with oven-roasted cherry tomatoes and tangy goat cheese and serve with drinks.

Heat the oven to 180°C/Gas 4. Toss the cherry tomatoes in olive oil and bake for 15 minutes until soft and squidgy. Remove and cool to room temperature.

To make the oatcakes, whiz the oats, flour, butter and salt in a food processor. Add water, 1 tbsp at a time, until the mixture starts to come together.

Push the dough together with your hands, then gently roll or pat it out on a lightly floured surface until 1 cm thick. Cut into 4 or 5 cm rounds with a pastry cutter or upturned liqueur glass. Re-roll the scraps and cut out more rounds.

Place the oatcakes on a non-stick baking sheet and bake for 10 to 12 minutes. Cool on a wire rack and store in an airtight container. Serve topped with a thin slice of goat cheese and a cherry tomato.

MAKES 20
20 cherry tomatoes
1 tbsp extra virgin olive oil
120 g rolled oats
100 g plain flour
80 g butter, softened
1 tsp sea salt
2–4 tbsp cold water
200 g fresh, firm goat cheese
(in a round log)

Coconut prawns with chilli

This is fast, simple, and comes with all those tangy tastes you love in Thai food. No time? Then use cooked prawns and add a little coconut milk to the dressing.

Devein the prawns by hooking a thin bamboo skewer through the spine and pulling out the black thread, but don't peel them. Heat the coconut milk, salt and water in a pan until simmering. Add the prawns and simmer for 3 to 4 minutes until they change colour. Remove and cool, then peel, leaving the tail intact.

Trim the lemongrass and finely slice the white section only. Finely slice the chillies and shallots. Cut the kaffir lime leaves (if using) into thin ribbons.

Combine the lemongrass, chillies, shallots, lime leaves or zest, mint and coriander in a bowl. Add the prawns and toss gently. Add the lime juice, fish sauce and 2 tbsp of the coconut broth, and toss lightly. Serve at room temperature, scattered with crushed peanuts.

SERVES 4
16 medium raw prawns
250 ml canned coconut milk
salt
250 ml water
1 lemongrass stalk
2 small red chillies
4 shallots, peeled
4 kaffir lime leaves, or 1 tsp grated lime zest
handful of mint leaves
handful of coriander leaves
2 tbsp lime juice
2 tbsp Thai fish sauce (nam pla)
2 tbsp salted peanuts, crushed

Belgian mussels

Mussels are easy. Just wash them well and pull out the little beards, discarding any that don't close when tapped. Serve with crusty bread and a pot of real mayonnaise for dipping.

Give the mussels a quick scrub; pull out the little beards and discard.

Peel the onion and slice into fine rings. Heat the butter and oil in a large lidded pan, and cook the onion gently for 5 minutes.

Add the white wine, chicken stock, celery and garlic cloves, and bring to the boil. Add the mussels, cover with the lid and cook for 1 minute, then shake the pan, remove the lid and take out the mussels that have opened.

Repeat this process a few times, discarding any mussels that refuse to open. Add the cream and parsley to the pan, and gently warm through, stirring.

Distribute the mussels among 4 warmed, deep soup bowls and pour the creamy broth on top.

SERVES 4

1.5kg mussels

1 onion

1 tbsp butter

1 tbsp olive oil

200ml dry white wine

250ml light chicken stock or
     water

2 celery stalks, finely sliced

2 garlic cloves, peeled and
     smashed

2 tbsp pouring cream

2 tbsp chopped parsley

simple brunches

Sweet onion crostini

If brunch is half breakfast, half lunch – and better than both – then this sweet, slow-cooked onion with Italian prosciutto on hot toast is perfect brunch material. You can use Spanish jamón serrano if you prefer.

Peel the onions and slice finely into rings. Melt the butter with the oil in a heavy-based fry pan, add the onions, sea salt, pepper and rosemary and cook gently for 20 minutes, tossing occasionally, until soft and translucent.

Turn up the heat, add the white wine, and allow it to bubble and reduce, stirring well. Lower the heat and cook for a further 10 to 15 minutes until the onions are soft and gooey. Add the wine vinegar, and toss well. You can leave the onions as they are, which I prefer, or purée them in a food processor and reheat the purée.

Toast or grill the bread on both sides. Pile a generous amount of sweet onions on the toast and top with folded slices of prosciutto. Tuck in the rosemary sprigs and serve.

SERVES 4

4 large white onions

1 tbsp butter

1 tbsp olive oil

sea salt

freshly ground black pepper

2 rosemary sprigs

250 ml white wine

1 tbsp red wine vinegar

4 thick slices sourdough bread

8 thin slices prosciutto

4 rosemary sprigs, to serve

Catalan tomato bread

Cut 4 big soft bread rolls in half and lightly grill. Brush with olive oil and rub with a cut garlic clove. Halve 4 ripe tomatoes and rub over the rolls, squeezing the juices and seeds into the bread. Grill until browned, and serve with egg dishes, cured meats and cheeses.

Amish pancakes

Soft, light oatmeal pancakes to stack high with crisp bacon or soft prosciutto, and drizzle with maple syrup.

Heat the milk to just below boiling point, remove from the heat, and add the rolled oats and sugar. Stir well, and leave to cool.

Sift the flour, baking powder and salt together into a large bowl, add the cooled mixture, and stir well. Beat the egg yolks lightly and stir into the mixture.

Beat the egg whites in a dry bowl until stiff and peaky, then lightly fold into the pancake batter.

Grill or pan-fry the bacon rashers (if using) until crisp, and drain on paper towel.

Heat a large non-stick fry pan and add a teaspoon of butter. Drop tablespoons of batter into the pan and cook over medium heat. When bubbles appear on top, turn and cook the other side until golden. Remove and keep warm. Add another teaspoon of butter, and repeat to cook the rest of the pancakes.

Serve 2 or 3 pancakes per person. Stack them with bacon or prosciutto and drizzle with maple syrup.

MAKES 12
400 ml milk
100 g rolled oats
1 tbsp sugar
1 tbsp plain flour
2 tsp baking powder
pinch of salt
2 large free-range eggs,
separated
8 thin rashers rindless bacon,
or 8 thin slices prosciutto
unsalted butter for frying
maple syrup or golden syrup,
to serve

Little egg and ham pies

Line each mould of a muffin tray with ham, crack an egg into it, add cream and a little grated cheese, and bake. Serve warm for brunch, or take on a picnic.

Heat the oven to 180°C/Gas 4. Lightly oil or butter a 12-hole muffin tray. Line the base and most of the sides of each mould with a slice of ham, then break an egg into the hollow. Drizzle with the cream, and scatter with sea salt, pepper, parsley and parmesan.

Bake for 15 to 20 minutes until the egg is just set and starting to shrink away from the sides of the tin. Leave to cool for 5 minutes, then run a knife around each mould to loosen the ham and egg, and remove to a wire tray. Eat warm, or at room temperature.

MAKES 12

1 tsp olive oil or butter

12 thin slices good quality ham

12 large free-range eggs

2 tbsp cream

sea salt

freshly ground black pepper

2 tbsp roughly chopped parsley

4 tbsp freshly grated parmesan

chicken pies

Chicken pies

Buy a ready-roasted chicken or a Chinatown soy chicken, and these simple, warm chicken pies are even simpler.

Heat the oven to 200°C/Gas 6. Soak the dried mushrooms in hot water to cover for 30 minutes. Strip the meat from the chicken and chop it finely.

Peel and finely chop the shallots. Drain the mushrooms, trim off the stalks and slice the caps finely.

Heat the oil in a pan, and cook the shallots gently until soft. Sprinkle with the flour and cook, stirring, for 2 minutes. Gradually add the chicken stock, stirring. Add the mushrooms, and soy, oyster and hoi sin sauces and simmer for 5 minutes. Remove from the heat, stir in the chicken and coriander, and leave to cool.

Roll out half the pastry and cut into twelve 12 cm squares. Repeat with the other half. Plop 1 tbsp of the chicken mixture on a pastry square, top with another square and press down around the filling to seal. Place a large upturned glass over the top, and trim the pie into a circle. Repeat until all pies are made.

Brush the pies with egg yolk, cut a small slash in the top, and bake for 20 to 25 minutes until golden.

MAKES 12

6 dried shiitake mushrooms

1 medium chicken, roasted
 or poached

4 shallots, or 1 small onion

2 tbsp groundnut or peanut oil

1 tbsp plain flour

250 ml chicken stock

1 tbsp soy sauce

1 tbsp oyster sauce

1 tbsp hoi sin or plum sauce

2 tbsp finely chopped coriander

500 g packet puff pastry

1 egg yolk, beaten with
 1 tbsp milk

Country terrine

A hearty, rustic country pâté to serve with crusty bread, little green cornichons and salad leaves.

Roughly chop the bacon, reserving 4 rashers for the top. Clean and trim the chicken livers, and roughly chop.

Combine the minced pork, bacon and chicken livers in a large bowl, along with the chopped herbs, shallots, garlic, salt, pepper, nutmeg and brandy. Mix well with your hands, then cover and leave in the refrigerator overnight.

Heat the oven to 180°C/Gas 4. Mix the egg into the meat and pile the mixture into a 1 litre ovenproof dish. Shape the top into a mound and cover with remaining bacon. Cover with a tight-fitting lid or foil, and bake for 1½ hours, or until the pâté starts to shrink away from the sides of the dish. Cool slightly, then drain off some of the fat. Serve at room temperature, topped with thyme sprigs.

SERVES 8

200g rindless streaky bacon, plus 4 extra rashers
250g chicken livers
1kg coarsely minced fatty pork
1 tbsp finely chopped parsley
1 tbsp finely chopped thyme
1 tbsp finely chopped sage
2 shallots, peeled and finely sliced
2 garlic cloves, peeled and crushed
2 tsp salt
½ tsp freshly ground black pepper
½ tsp freshly grated nutmeg
2 tbsp brandy or port
1 large free-range egg, beaten
thyme sprigs, to serve

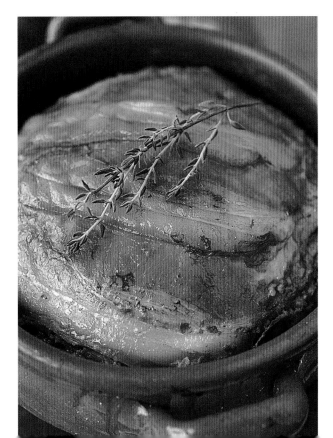

Figs and baked ricotta

Place 500 g fresh ricotta in a baking dish. Scatter with sea salt, pepper, thyme and rosemary, drizzle with extra virgin olive oil and bake at 200°C/Gas 6 for 15 minutes.
Add 6 halved ripe figs and bake for another 10 minutes.
Serve with prosciutto, drizzled with olive oil and balsamic vinegar.

Egyptian beetroot dip

Whiz 5 cooked, peeled beetroot in a blender with 300 ml yoghurt, 2 crushed garlic cloves, 2 tbsp lemon juice, 2 tbsp extra virgin olive oil, sea salt, pepper and ½ tsp each of ground cumin, coriander, paprika and cinnamon. Serve with warm flat bread for dipping.

Two fruity drinks

Icy cold, silky smooth and highly energizing, a frozen Indian lassi is sheer liquid food. Or if you have a juice extractor, try the wake-up juice below.

SERVES 4

3 bananas, peeled

100g red berries

200ml plain low-fat yoghurt

1 tbsp runny honey

250ml orange juice

Place the bananas in a plastic bag and freeze for an hour or two until firm. Whiz the bananas, berries, yoghurt, honey and orange juice together in a blender until smooth and creamy.

Adjust the sweetness (add more honey if the berries are tart) and thickness (add more orange juice to thin the drink if needed). Serve the lassi in chilled glasses.

SERVES 4

1 beetroot

3 green-skinned apples

1cm cube of fresh ginger

Scrub the beetroot, apples and ginger clean, and cut into segments small enough to fit into your juice extractor. Juice the beetroot first, then the ginger and finally, the apples, which will help clear the machine of the beetroot. Dilute the wake-up juice with cold filtered water to taste.

Tunisian salad rolls

One of the world's crunchiest, freshest salads. Serve it with lightly warmed pitta bread, or stuff it into the pitta pocket and eat in your hands.

Finely chop the sweet red pepper, discarding the core and seeds. Cut the tomatoes in half, squeeze out and discard the seeds and juice, and finely chop the flesh. Finely chop the radishes, spring onions and hard-boiled eggs.

Combine the red pepper, tomatoes, radishes, spring onions, eggs, capers and tuna in a large bowl.

Whisk the lemon juice, olive oil, sea salt, pepper, coriander and caraway together. Pour this spiced oil over the salad and toss well.

Lightly warm the pitta breads in the oven or under the grill, then cut off the top 1cm. Fill the pitta pockets with the salad and serve.

SERVES 4
1 sweet red pepper
2 tomatoes
2 small radishes
2 spring onions
2 hard-boiled eggs, peeled
1 tbsp tiny capers, rinsed
300g canned tuna
in oil, drained
8 pitta breads

Spiced oil:
2 tsp lemon juice
1 tbsp olive oil
sea salt
freshly ground black pepper
$\frac{1}{2}$ tsp ground coriander
$\frac{1}{2}$ tsp ground caraway

aromatic, cheeky herbs

Variety isn't the spice of life, after all - it's the herb. Change the herb and you alter the smell, the taste and the look of your food. Simple, really.

bite into a fresh herb sandwich

Finely snip a handful of chives and mix with some finely chopped mint, parsley and thyme. Sandwich between slices of fresh white bread, spread with cream cheese or fresh ricotta spiked with sea salt and black pepper.

add fresh mint to your salad greens

Add a handful of fresh mint leaves to your next green leaf salad, dress it with 2 tbsp extra virgin olive oil, 1 tbsp red wine vinegar, sea salt, pepper and 1 tsp Dijon mustard, and every mouthful will taste wild.

add fragrance to fruit

Fruits love herbs, not just spices. Add basil to fresh ripe peaches and pineapple. Chop fresh mint and papaya and toss with a squeeze of lime juice and a little sugar. Poach stone fruit in a light sugar syrup with bay leaves and peppercorns.

a simple way with sage

Fry sage leaves in olive oil until crisp, then remove. Use the oil to pan-fry mushrooms, potatoes, crumbed veal, pork chops or duck breasts. Serve topped with the crisp-fried sage leaves.

give the knife a rest

You don't always have to chop fresh herbs. Chives are better snipped with scissors, and basil leaves are better simply torn. Throw whole parsley, sage and oregano leaves into pasta sauces, soups and stews, and strew whole sprigs of thyme and rosemary over roasts.

add a herb crust to fish
Mix 2 tbsp chopped basil, parsley and chervil with a cupful of soft breadcrumbs, salt, pepper, a pinch of cayenne and a squeeze of lime juice. Dip 4 fish fillets into beaten egg, then into the herb crumbs, and fry until crisp and golden.

marinate everything in sight
Marinate lamb chops with rosemary or oregano in olive oil before grilling. Marinate chicken in coriander, mint, basil and vegetable oil before barbecuing. Marinate sliced tomatoes and goat cheese in thyme, garlic and olive oil, and serve all summer long.

bay-leaf your meatballs
Make your favourite bite-sized meatballs, wrap a lightly oiled bay leaf around each one and secure with a wooden cocktail stick or toothpick. Bake and serve, but don't eat the leaf.

zap your potato salad
Chives are the obvious pick, but try spiking potato salad with a gremolata – 2 crushed garlic cloves tossed with 2 tbsp finely chopped parsley and 1 tbsp grated lemon rind – and prepare to be amazed. Scatter the same gremolata over pan-fried fish, parmesan risotto, roast chicken, and baked mushrooms.

make a pot of herb tea
Add boiling water to a handful of crushed mint or basil, or a few stems of bashed lemongrass and leave to steep for 5 minutes. Strain and serve with a sprig of the same herb.

simple lunches

Warm Mediterranean veg

A meal in itself for vegetable lovers, or a simple, colourful accompaniment to fish, sausages, lamb or chicken.

Heat the oven to 180°C/Gas 4. Cut the onion in half and slice finely. Cut the red and yellow peppers into long strips, discarding the core and seeds.

Heat the 1 tbsp oil in a fry pan, and fry the onion and peppers for 10 minutes until they start to soften. Slice the courgettes and tomatoes into rings.

Arrange the onion and peppers in the base of a lightly oiled baking tin or gratin dish, and layer the sliced courgettes and tomatoes on top – in any order you like.

Mix the extra virgin olive oil with the lemon juice, garlic, rosemary, thyme, sea salt and pepper. Drizzle over the vegetables and bake for about 1 hour until tender. Serve hot or warm.

SERVES 4

1 onion, peeled

1 sweet red pepper

1 sweet yellow pepper

1 tbsp olive oil

4 medium courgettes
(zucchini)

4 Roma tomatoes

2 tbsp extra virgin olive oil

1 tbsp lemon juice

1 garlic clove, peeled and
crushed

4 rosemary sprigs

6 thyme sprigs

sea salt

freshly ground black pepper

Couscous with dates

Golden couscous makes a light and healthy lunch, with a spicy, fragrant broth and some simple steamed vegetables.

Heat the oven to 160°C/Gas 3. Place the couscous in a large heatproof bowl and pour the boiling water on top. Add the olive oil and diced butter, and toss them through with a fork. Cover and place in the oven for 15 minutes.

Meanwhile, finely slice the onions. Heat the oil in a pan and fry the onions until soft. Add the garlic, tomatoes, sugar, salt, pepper, saffron, paprika, ginger and parsley, and simmer for 10 minutes.

Steam or lightly boil the courgettes, dried apricots and dates for 5 minutes, then drain and thickly slice the courgettes.

Run a fork through the couscous to break up any lumps and season with salt. Pile into warm bowls and top with the courgettes, apricots and dates. Serve, with the hot tomato broth to the side.

SERVES 4

Couscous:
500g couscous
500ml boiling water
1 tbsp olive oil
1 tbsp butter, diced

Vegetables and broth:
2 onions, peeled
2 tbsp olive oil
2 garlic cloves, peeled and crushed
400g canned chopped tomatoes
1 tsp sugar
sea salt
freshly ground black pepper
$\frac{1}{2}$ tsp powdered saffron
1 tsp paprika
1 tsp ground ginger
2 tbsp chopped parsley
6 courgettes (zucchini), green and yellow
12 dried apricots
10 moist, dried dates, pitted and sliced

Lamb steak sandwich

This is even nicer than the more traditional steak sandwich, as lamb teams with sweetly caramelised onions for a hearty weekend lunch.

Heat the oven to 180°C/Gas 4. Finely slice the onions and toss in a roasting pan with 2 tbsp olive oil, the balsamic vinegar, salt and pepper. Bake for 30 to 40 minutes until caramelised.

Flatten each lamb fillet or steak with a meat mallet, then cut in two. Combine the extra virgin olive oil, white wine, garlic and oregano in a shallow dish, add the lamb and coat well.

Slice the tomatoes and season with salt and pepper. Beat the mustard into the mayonnaise.

Lightly oil a non-stick fry pan and heat. When it is very hot, add the lamb and sear until crusty, turning once. This will only take a minute or two either side. Season well, and set aside while you toast or grill the bread.

Spread 4 toast slices with the mustard mayonnaise, and arrange the rocket leaves, tomatoes, lamb and caramelised onions on top. Top with the remaining toast slices.

SERVES 4
3 white onions
2 tbsp olive oil
2 tbsp balsamic vinegar
sea salt
freshly ground black pepper
4 lamb fillets or boneless leg steaks, around 180g each
2 tbsp extra virgin olive oil
2 tbsp white wine
1 garlic clove, smashed
1 tbsp oregano leaves
4 vine-ripened tomatoes
1 tbsp Dijon mustard
200g good mayonnaise
8 thick slices sourdough or light rye bread
200g baby rocket leaves

Haloumi, tomato and beans

Fresh haloumi is a rich, salty Greek-Cypriot cheese sold pre-packed in plastic, with a little brine.

Heat the oven to 180°C/Gas 4. Cut the tomatoes in half lengthwise and arrange in a baking tin. Drizzle with 1 tbsp olive oil, sea salt, pepper and thyme, and bake for 30 minutes until soft.

Cook the green beans in simmering salted water for 5 minutes.

Rinse the haloumi, then cut into slices, a little less than 1 cm thick. Heat the remaining olive oil in a non-stick fry pan and, when hot, sizzle the haloumi slices until golden brown. Turn briefly and sizzle the other side.

Whisk the lemon juice, olive oil, capers and parsley together. Drain the beans and toss in the dressing. Arrange the tomatoes and beans on 4 dinner plates, and top with haloumi. Drizzle with the dressing and serve, with lemon.

SERVES 4

8 plum tomatoes

2 tbsp olive oil

sea salt

freshly ground black pepper

few thyme sprigs

400g green beans, topped

400g haloumi

1 lemon, quartered

Dressing:

1 tbsp lemon juice

2 tbsp extra virgin olive oil

1 tbsp capers, rinsed

1 tbsp chopped parsley

sizzle haloumi until golden

French café salad

You can make a different café salad every day – from eggs, potatoes and tuna, or chicken, beans and tomato, or asparagus, avocado and ham – you get the idea.

Heat the oven to 200°C/Gas 6. Cut the tomatoes in half and arrange on a baking tray. Season with sea salt and pepper, drizzle with 1 tbsp olive oil and bake for 20 minutes.

Cook the potatoes and beans in simmering salted water until tender. Drain and cut the potatoes in half. Peel the hard-boiled eggs and cut into quarters.

Heat 1 tbsp olive oil in a non-stick fry pan and sear the tuna steaks for 3 minutes on each side, leaving the inside pink.

To make the dressing, in a large bowl whisk the wine vinegar, olive oil and mustard with sea salt and pepper until thick.

Dress the rocket leaves, potatoes, beans and olives and arrange on dinner plates with the tomatoes and eggs. Cut the tuna into chunks and place on top, with the anchovy fillets.

SERVES 4

4 plum tomatoes

sea salt

freshly ground black pepper

2 tbsp olive oil

8 small potatoes, peeled

250g fine green beans, trimmed

4 hard-boiled eggs

2 fresh tuna steaks, around 300g each, trimmed

200g rocket or spinach leaves

2 tbsp small black olives

4 anchovy fillets, halved

Dressing:

2 tbsp red wine vinegar

4 tbsp extra virgin olive oil

1 tsp Dijon mustard

beetroot burgers

spanish meatballs

Beetroot burgers

Australians love beetroot with their burgers, but this idea is actually from Sweden, where beetroot is added to the meat to give it a sweet tang.

Finely chop the onion. Heat the butter and olive oil in a fry pan and cook the onion slowly until pale and soft, then cool.

Combine the minced beef, egg yolks, capers, sea salt and pepper in a bowl, add the onion and mix together thoroughly. Add the pickled beetroot and juice, and mix well. With wet hands, shape the mixture into 4 large, flat burgers (the traditional method) or make 8 smaller, taller patties.

Heat a ridged cast-iron grill pan, oil it and the burgers lightly, and cook them on a medium heat for about 5 minutes each side. (Alternatively heat a little olive oil in a fry pan and cook the burgers over medium heat until brown on each side.)

Meanwhile, toast the muffins. Serve the burgers in the toasted muffins, with a little salad of green leaves, or with wilted spinach and small boiled potatoes.

SERVES 4

1 onion, peeled

1 tbsp butter

1 tbsp olive oil

500 g minced beef

2 egg yolks

1 tbsp capers, rinsed and
 chopped

sea salt

freshly ground black pepper

3 tbsp pickled beetroot,
 finely chopped

1 tbsp pickled beetroot juice

4 English muffins

Spanish meatballs

Do this ahead of time and serve as a lazy, light lunch with some salad and the Catalan tomato bread on page 29.

Trim off the crusts and soak the bread in the milk for 5 minutes, then squeeze dry. Using your hands, mix the bread with the meat, garlic, nutmeg, parsley, egg, salt and pepper. Form the mixture into small balls, the size of a walnut, and roll in the flour.

Chop the onion. Cut the green pepper into strips, discarding the seeds.

Heat the olive oil in a heavy-based fry pan, and cook the meatballs in batches until well browned on all sides. Remove and add a little extra oil to the pan. Add the onion and green pepper and cook, stirring, for 5 minutes.

Return the meatballs to the pan, and add the chopped tomatoes, green olives, salt, pepper, sherry and stock. Bring to the boil, then simmer for 30 to 45 minutes until the sauce has reduced and thickened to a sludge. Serve hot.

MAKES 30
2 thick slices stale bread
125 ml milk
500 g minced lamb or beef
1 garlic clove, peeled and crushed
$\frac{1}{2}$ tsp freshly grated nutmeg
1 tbsp finely chopped parsley
1 free-range egg
sea salt
freshly ground black pepper
2 tbsp plain flour
1 onion, peeled
$\frac{1}{2}$ sweet green pepper
2 tbsp olive oil
800 g canned chopped tomatoes
12 green Spanish olives
3 tbsp dry sherry
250 ml chicken stock

Honey soy quail

Although it is baked in the oven, this crisp-skinned quail tastes as if it has been barbecued over hot coals in Chinatown, which is exactly how you want it to taste.

Wash the quail and pat dry. Tuck the wing tips in behind the body, and tie the legs together with string. Mix the honey and soy sauce in a bowl, add the quail and coat well. Leave to marinate for 30 minutes. Mix the five-spice powder with the salt and set aside.

Heat the oven to 200°C/Gas 6. Drain the quail, place in a baking tin and drizzle with the sesame oil. Bake the quail for 30 minutes, turning them around once or twice, until the meat is cooked and the skin is crisp and browned.

Serve on a bed of wilted spring onions or spinach, or with the sesame mangetout (snow peas) on page 78. Sprinkle with the five-spiced salt and serve with sweet chilli sauce.

SERVES 4

4 fresh quail, around
200g each
2 tbsp honey
3 tbsp soy sauce
1 tsp five-spice powder
1 tsp salt
1 tsp sesame oil
2 tbsp sweet, seedy Thai
chilli sauce

Parmesan lamb cutlets

I've always loved crumbed lamb cutlets, either hot with mashed potato and peas, or cold on a picnic with a spicy tomato relish. These cutlets have a cheese crumb that makes them even nicer.

Flatten the meat with a meat mallet, leaving it on the bone. Put the flour, salt and pepper in a plastic bag, and toss each chop in the flour, shaking off any excess.

Place the eggs in a shallow bowl, and mix the parmesan and breadcrumbs together in another one.

SERVES 4

12 lamb cutlets, well trimmed

2 tbsp plain flour

sea salt

freshly ground black pepper

2 free-range eggs, beaten

2 tbsp finely grated parmesan

4 tbsp dried breadcrumbs

2 tbsp light olive oil

1 tbsp butter

1 lemon, quartered

Heat the oil and butter in a large heavy-based fry pan. Dip each chop in the beaten egg, then in the parmesan crumbs to coat, and fry over medium heat on both sides until crisp and golden brown.

Drain the crumbed cutlets on paper towel. Serve with lemon, and a sharply dressed green salad.

Mixed grill

When I was growing up in Australia, a mixed grill was the best pub lunch around. This is a bit classier, but just as good.

Cut the steak into 4 pieces. Prick the sausages, and cut bacon rashers in half. Heat a ridged cast-iron grill pan or barbecue.

Cut the courgettes on the diagonal into 1cm slices. Cut the tomatoes in half lengthwise. Brush the courgettes and tomatoes with olive oil and grill or barbecue until soft.

Brush the sausages with olive oil and grill until browned. Fry the bacon in a non-stick fry pan until crisp. Brush the steaks with olive oil and grill for around 3 minutes on one side, then 1 minute on the other, depending on thickness.

Wash the spinach and shake dry. Whisk the olive oil, vinegar, mustard, sea salt and pepper together until thick, dress the leaves and arrange on plates. Top with the grilled vegetables and meats.

SERVES 4
300g beef fillet (eg Scotch),
3cm thick
12 short, spicy beef chipolata
sausages
4 thin rashers rindless bacon
2 courgettes (zucchini)
4 plum tomatoes
1 tbsp olive oil
100g baby spinach leaves

Dressing:
2 tbsp extra virgin olive oil
1 tbsp red wine vinegar
1 tsp Dijon mustard
sea salt
freshly ground black pepper

simple salads

Yellow pepper salad

Put these warm, sunny flavours with sliced prosciutto and fresh crusty bread for a lazy lunch, or with barbecued fish, chicken or lamb at any time.

Heat the oven to 200°C/Gas 6. Place the peppers in a baking tin and coat with a little of the olive oil. Bake for 20 minutes, turning once or twice, until lightly scorched. Alternatively you can grill the oiled peppers on a cast-iron grill pan, or under the grill.

Remove peppers from the heat and place in a bowl. Cover and leave for 10 minutes, then peel away the skin, and remove the core and seeds. Cut the flesh lengthwise into thick strips.

Arrange the pepper strips on a serving plate. Combine the olives, remaining olive oil, sea salt and pepper, and drizzle over the top. Scatter with basil leaves or sprigs of thyme.

SERVES 4

2 yellow and 2 orange peppers
   (or 4 yellow ones)
2 tbsp extra virgin olive oil
2 tbsp small black olives
sea salt
freshly ground black pepper
few basil leaves, or thyme
   sprigs

Grilled courgette salad

Slice 6 courgettes (zucchini) lengthwise, brush with olive oil and grill. Whisk 2 tbsp each lemon juice, extra virgin olive oil and chopped dill. Season and pour over the courgettes. Serve topped with grilled lemon.

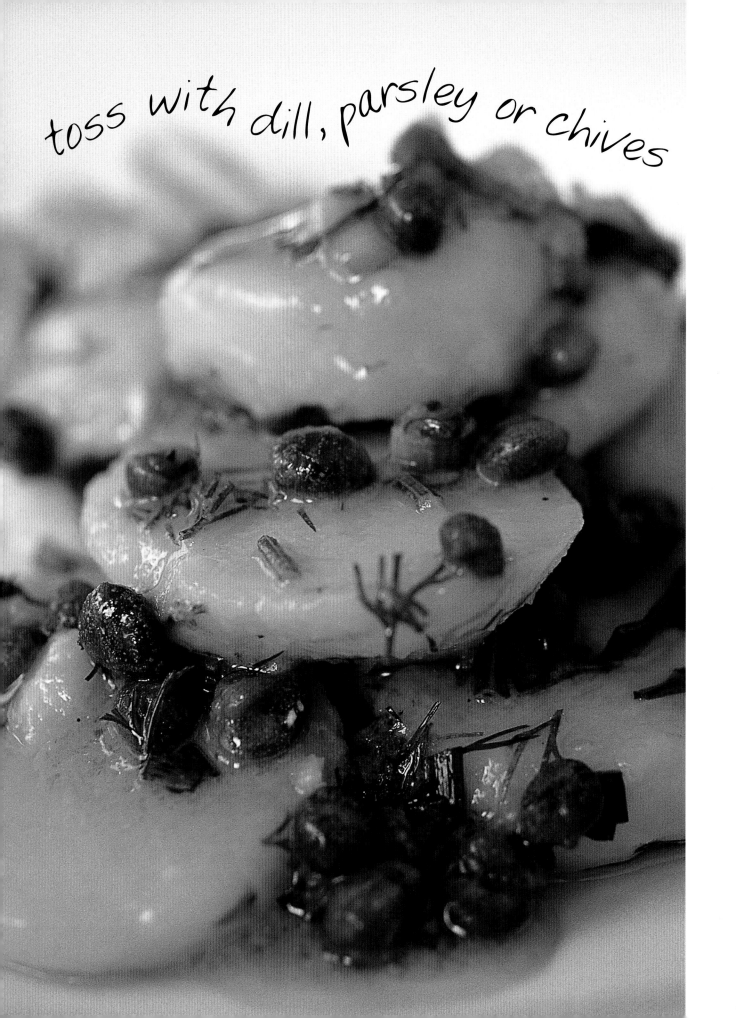

toss with dill, parsley or chives

Warm potatoes and capers

Cold potatoes are an abomination, but something quite special happens when warm potatoes hit a generous, mustardy dressing. Eat warm, obviously.

Cook the potatoes in simmering, salted water until tender but still firm, about 20 minutes. Finely chop the spring onions.

In the meantime, make the dressing. Combine the olive oil, wine vinegar, mustard, sea salt and pepper in a large bowl and whisk well until thickened. Add the capers, spring onions and chopped herbs, and toss lightly.

Drain the potatoes and slice them thickly, as soon as you can handle them. Toss them carefully in the dressing, making sure the slices don't stick together. Arrange on warmed plates, drizzle with any extra dressing and serve.

SERVES 4
6 medium waxy potatoes,
peeled
3 spring onions
1 tbsp small capers, rinsed
2 tbsp chopped dill, parsley
or chives

Dressing:
3 tbsp extra virgin olive oil
2 tbsp red wine vinegar
1 tsp Dijon mustard
sea salt
freshly ground black pepper

Chorizo and sweet potato

Cut 2 cooked sweet potatoes and 4 chorizo sausages thickly on the diagonal, brush with oil and grill until sizzling. Whisk 1 tbsp lemon juice and 2 tbsp olive oil with 1 tbsp chopped parsley, then toss with 200 g rocket leaves. Pile the sizzling sweet potatoes and sausages on top.

Fattoush

This crunchy Syrian salad combines crisp grilled bread with fresh, juicy, summery flavours. It's startlingly good with prawns, lobster or crab.

Heat the grill. Open up the flat bread until you have two rounds, and grill lightly until crisp and golden. Crumble into small shards with your hands, and set aside.

Peel the cucumbers, cut in half lengthwise, and scoop out and discard the seeds. Halve the tomatoes and scoop out the seeds and juice. Chop the cucumbers, tomatoes, sweet pepper, radishes and spring onions, and mix with the parsley and mint.

Whisk the olive oil, lemon juice, cinnamon, sea salt and pepper together. Toss the salad in the dressing, add the crisp bread and toss again. Using a slotted spoon, divide the salad between 4 individual plates, or pile onto one big platter.

SERVES 4

1 round of Lebanese flat bread, or 2 pitta breads

2 small Lebanese cucumbers

2 ripe tomatoes

1/2 sweet red pepper

4 small radishes

6 spring onions

3 tbsp finely chopped parsley

3 tbsp finely chopped mint

Dressing:

4 tbsp olive oil

3 tbsp lemon juice

1/2 tsp ground cinnamon

sea salt

freshly ground black pepper

parsley and lemon salad

Sesame mangetout

Mangetout (snow peas) are too boring for words when cooked whole. But shred them finely and toss raw in a sweet Asian vinaigrette, and they taste wild. Serve as a salad or side dish, or use as a base for seafood, duck or barbecued quail.

Wash and dry the mangetout, then finely slice lengthwise into matchsticks, using the tip of a sharp knife. This will take some time, but keep going and don't curse me too much. The effect it has on the flavour and texture is too great to give up now.

For the dressing, mix the sugar, soy sauce, wine vinegar, rice wine and sesame oil together. Lightly toss the shredded mangetout in the dressing, draining off any excess.

SERVES 4

250g mangetout (snow peas)

2 tsp sesame seeds

Dressing:

1 tsp sugar

1 tbsp soy sauce

1 tbsp rice wine vinegar, or
   white wine vinegar

1 tbsp Chinese rice wine, or
   dry sherry

2 tsp sesame oil

Arrange the dressed mangetout on a serving plate and sprinkle with the sesame seeds to serve.

Parsley and lemon salad

The freshest, brightest, herbiest, tangiest salad around, traditionally eaten wrapped in fresh, unsprayed, vine leaves. It's never as good as when you first make it, so eat soon after.

Rinse the burghul, then soak in cold water to cover for 1 hour, or until swollen.

Chop the spring onions. Peel the cucumber, halve, scoop out the seeds and finely chop the flesh. Cut the tomatoes in half, squeeze out and discard the seeds and juice, and dice the flesh.

Pick off the herb leaves, wash and dry well, then roughly chop. Drain the burghul and squeeze dry. Toss with the herbs, spring onions, cucumber and tomato.

Mix the olive oil with the lemon juice, cumin, cayenne and sea salt. Pour the dressing over the salad, toss well and serve.

SERVES 4

150g fine burghul
(bulgur wheat)
2 spring onions
1 small cucumber
2 tomatoes
2 bunches of parsley
1 bunch of mint

Dressing:
2 tbsp extra virgin olive oil
2 tbsp lemon juice
$\frac{1}{2}$ tsp ground cumin
$\frac{1}{2}$ tsp cayenne pepper
1 tsp sea salt

Chicken Caesar

It's the most popular thing on the café menu, but we can do it better at home. Note this dressing contains raw egg yolk.

To make the dressing, whiz the egg yolk, garlic, anchovy fillets, mustard, wine vinegar, white wine, salt and pepper in a blender until smooth. With the motor running, gradually add the olive oil.

Heat the grill. Brush the chicken with olive oil and grill gently for 15 minutes, turning once, or until cooked through. Season the chicken with salt and pepper and slice thickly. Grill or fry the bacon until crisp, then crumble into shards.

Grill or toast the bread, then brush with a little olive oil and cut into cubes to make croûtons. Remove the outer lettuce leaves.

Combine the inner lettuce leaves with the croûtons, chicken and half the dressing in a large bowl. Toss gently, then arrange on serving plates. Scatter with the bacon and parmesan, and drizzle with the remaining dressing.

SERVES 4

3 chicken breast fillets

1–2 tbsp extra virgin olive oil

4 rashers rindless bacon

2 thick slices sourdough bread

4 Little Gem lettuces, or 2 Cos

1 tbsp freshly grated parmesan

Dressing:

1 egg yolk

2 garlic cloves, peeled

2 anchovy fillets

1 tsp Dijon mustard

2 tbsp white wine vinegar

1 tbsp white wine

sea salt

freshly ground black pepper

125 ml light olive oil

Asian duck salad

Buy half a Chinese roast duck in Chinatown or use leftover roast duck, and turn it into a light, fresh, crunchy salad with a delicate, sweet dressing. Also good with barbecued chicken.

Slice or shred the duck meat, discarding the bones. Cut the carrots into short lengths, then into matchsticks. Slice the mangetout, sweet pepper and spring onions lengthwise into matchsticks.

Put the carrots, pepper and bean sprouts in a bowl, pour a jug of boiling water over them, then drain and refresh under cold running water. Drain again.

To make the dressing, whisk the mirin, rice vinegar, fish sauce, sugar, salt, pepper and olive oil together in a bowl.

Add the vegetables and duck to the dressing and toss gently. Pile onto plates and serve, with or without steamed rice.

SERVES 4
½ Chinese roast duck, or
leftover roast duck
2 carrots, peeled
200 g mangetout (snow peas)
1 sweet red or yellow pepper,
cored and seeded
2 spring onions, trimmed
200 g bean sprouts

Dressing:
1 tbsp mirin (Japanese
sweet rice wine)
2 tbsp Japanese rice vinegar
1 tbsp fish sauce
1 tsp sugar
sea salt
freshly ground black pepper
3 tbsp olive oil

juicy, fruity tomatoes

Smash them, sizzle them, slice them, or eat them out of your hand.

Tomatoes add instant flavour, acidity, juicy bits,

and film star colour.

buy the perfect tomato

Buy tomatoes that are good enough to eat in your hands:
taut-skinned, green-stemmed, perfumed, ripened on the vine
before picking, and brought to the market with stalks intact,
which helps them last longer.

how to peel and seed

Cut out the core, and cut a small cross in the base. Drop the
tomatoes into a pot of simmering water for 20 seconds, then
remove, run under cold water, and slip off the skins. Cut in half,
squeeze out and discard the seeds and the juice.

instant tomato sauce

Sizzle a punnet of whole cherry tomatoes with a spoonful of
olive oil in a hot non-stick fry pan until the skins burst, then tip
the lot over green beans or asparagus, grilled fish, or pan-fried
chicken breast – instant sauce.

simple tomato vinaigrette

Peel, seed and dice 2 tomatoes and stir gently through 4 tbsp
extra virgin olive oil and 1 tbsp red wine vinegar, sea salt and
pepper. Spoon over grilled sea bass or pan-fried salmon.

soft and juicy semi-dried tomatoes

Cut 1kg plum tomatoes lengthwise into three. Arrange on a
rack over a tray, sprinkle with sea salt and thyme, and bake at
60°C overnight until semi-dried. Cool, layer in a sterilised jar,
top with olive oil, seal and keep refrigerated.

intensify the flavour
Baking reduces water content, and concentrates flavour and acidity. Just cut tomatoes in half, drizzle with olive oil, scatter with sea salt and pepper and bake at 180°C/Gas 4 for 30 to 40 minutes or until they smell interesting.

hot and cold pasta sauce
Peel, seed and roughly chop 4 ripe red tomatoes and douse in extra virgin olive oil with a few smashed garlic cloves and a handful of basil leaves. Leave for a few hours to intensify, then toss the lot through hot linguine.

fast tomato tart
Roll out puff pastry, cut into saucer shapes, brush with egg, prick and bake at 220°C/Gas 7 for 5 minutes. Cover each tart with halved cherry tomatoes tossed in olive oil, basil, sea salt and pepper and bake for 15 minutes until golden.

the 10 minute trick
Add a handful of cherry tomatoes to the last 10 minutes of cooking just about anything – parmesan risotto, Spanish rice, roast leg of lamb – they will turn ruby red, soft and juicy.

easy tomato jam
Seed and chop 1kg tomatoes. Gently simmer for 1 hour with 3 tbsp brown sugar, 1 tbsp mustard seeds, 2 tbsp red wine vinegar and 3 tbsp olive oil until thick and jammy. Season and cool, then store in airtight jars in the fridge.

simple dinners

Roast pesto chicken

This is a good trick: stuff pesto and breadcrumbs under the skin to protect the chicken breast from drying out, and you also infuse it with warm peppery basil.

Heat the oven to 200°C/Gas 6. Wash the chicken breasts and pat dry. Combine the pesto and breadcrumbs in a small bowl to make a thick paste, adding a little olive oil if it's too dry.

Work your fingers in between the skin and meat to create a space, leaving the skin attached at one end or along one side. Stuff the pesto mixture under the skin to cover the breast, carefully draw the skin back over it, and reshape.

Heat a non-stick fry pan, add 1 tbsp oil and sear the chicken skin for a minute or two until lightly golden, then place the chicken skin-side up on a baking tray and drizzle with remaining olive oil, lemon juice, sea salt and pepper.

Bake for about 20 minutes, depending on size, until cooked through. Rest for 5 minutes before serving, with a rocket or watercress salad.

SERVES 4

4 chicken breasts with skin, around 200g each

2 tbsp pesto

2 tbsp fine dry breadcrumbs

2 tbsp extra virgin olive oil

1 tbsp lemon juice

sea salt

freshly ground black pepper

Chicken tikka

Yes, you can make Punjabi-style chicken tikka without investing in a tandoor oven. For the best flavour, use leg or thigh rather than breast meat.

Cut the meat into cubes, about 5 cm square. Combine the yoghurt, lemon juice, garlic, ginger, spices, salt and vegetable oil in a non-reactive bowl, and mix well. Add the chicken, toss well and leave to marinate for 2 to 3 hours.

Heat the grill. Skewer the chicken pieces loosely on thin bamboo skewers, and place on a lightly oiled grill rack. Grill the chicken under a medium heat for about 5 minutes on each side, until nicely scorched and cooked through. (Alternatively you can place the rack over a baking tray and bake in a preheated oven at 230°C/Gas 8 for 10 to 12 minutes.)

Scatter with coriander or parsley, and serve the chicken tikka with lemon wedges and basmati rice.

SERVES 4
450 g boneless chicken meat
150 g yoghurt
2 tbsp lemon juice
2 garlic cloves, peeled and crushed
1 tbsp finely grated fresh ginger
2 tsp garam masala
$\frac{1}{2}$ tsp ground cumin
1 tsp paprika
$\frac{1}{2}$ tsp cayenne powder
1 tsp salt
2 tbsp vegetable oil
handful of coriander or parsley
lemon wedges, to serve

Pork with apple and sage

Top a seared pork chop with a juicy baked apple, and you have an instant fresh apple sauce on the plate.

Heat the oven to 180°C/Gas 4. Finely chop the onion. Mash 1 tbsp butter with the chopped onion, sugar and 4 sage leaves. Core the apples from the bottom, leaving the stalk intact at the top. Fill each hollow with the stuffing.

Stand the apples in a small baking tin, add the white wine, then pour in enough boiling water to come halfway up the side of the apples. Bake for 45 minutes, or until soft and squishy.

Heat the olive oil and remaining 1 tbsp butter in a heavy-based fry pan with 4 sage leaves. Add the pork chops and cook over moderate heat for around 8 to 10 minutes. Season well with sea salt and pepper. Turn the chops and cook for another 5 minutes or until tender.

Place the pork chops on warmed plates, top with the baked apples and tuck in the remaining sage leaves. Serve with mash.

SERVES 4

½ onion, peeled

2 tbsp butter

1 tbsp sugar

12 sage leaves

4 crisp, tart eating apples (eg Granny Smith)

250 ml dry white wine

1 tbsp olive oil

4 thick pork loin chops

sea salt

freshly ground black pepper

instant apple sauce

Beef sukiyaki

This isn't the traditional cook-at-the-table dish, but a quick dinner of beef and cellophane noodles. These thin, dried, white noodles are made from mung bean flour – you will find them in oriental food stores.

Pour boiling water over the noodles to cover them and let stand for 3 minutes. Cut the tofu into cubes. Finely chop the spring onions and white onion. Slice the beef as finely as you can.

In a small pan, combine the water and dashi powder, then add the soy sauce, mirin and sugar and heat gently, stirring. Rinse the soaked noodles in cold water, drain and set aside.

Heat half the oil in a heavy-based fry pan, and cook all the onions until soft. Add the noodles, tofu, spinach and dashi sauce, bring to the boil and simmer for 2 to 3 minutes.

Heat the remaining oil in a second fry pan until hot, and sear the beef slices for a few seconds until just cooked but still pink. Divide the noodle mixture between warmed bowls or plates and top with the seared beef. Serve with rice.

SERVES 4
200g cellophane noodles
200g fresh tofu
4 spring onions
1 white onion, peeled
400g best beef fillet
125ml water
10g instant dashi powder
3 tbsp soy sauce
3 tbsp mirin (Japanese sweet rice wine)
1 tbsp sugar
2 tbsp groundnut or peanut oil
200g spinach leaves, well rinsed

aubergine and lamb

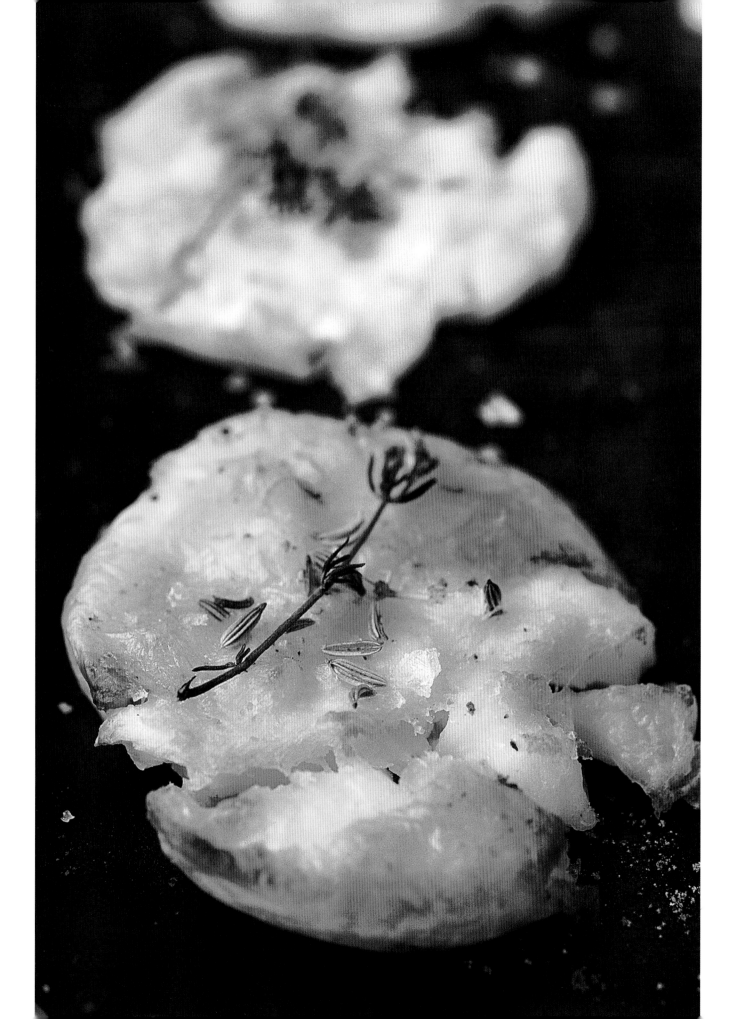

Aubergine and lamb

Lamb fillets are much more interesting if they are bashed flat and quickly seared, leaving them nice and juicy inside.

Flatten the lamb with a meat mallet. Mix 2 tbsp olive oil with the lemon juice, rosemary and thyme, and use to coat the lamb.

Heat the grill. Slice each aubergine lengthwise into eight 1cm thin, flat slices. Brush with olive oil, season with salt and pepper, and grill on both sides until scorched and tender.

Meanwhile, remove spinach stalks and wash the leaves well. Stuff the wet leaves into a saucepan and cook gently, covered, without any extra water, for a few minutes until wilted. Drain and keep warm.

Heat the grill, or a cast-iron grill pan or heavy-based fry pan, until hot. Cook the lamb for 2 minutes on either side (1 minute for small fillets). Season well, and rest on a warm plate.

Gently squeeze the spinach dry, and toss with a little olive oil, salt and pepper. Place a grilled aubergine slice on each warmed plate. Top with spinach, more aubergine, then lamb, and finally spinach. Spoon the pesto on top and serve.

SERVES 4

4 lamb fillets or boneless leg
   steaks, around 180g each
   (or eight 100g fillets)
3–4 tbsp extra virgin olive oil
1 tbsp lemon juice
3 rosemary sprigs
10 thyme sprigs
2 large aubergines (eggplant)
sea salt
freshly ground black pepper
1kg spinach (not baby)
2 tbsp pesto

Crash hot potatoes

This is one of those crazy little recipes that once tried, is immediately incorporated into your own repertoire. It's what you want when you want a crisp, roast potato, only better. And all you have to do is boil some small potatoes, smash them flat and blast them in a hot oven until they are terminally crisp. Serve with aubergine and lamb (see left), pan-fried fish, grilled sausages, or even on their own, with drinks.

Heat the oven to 250°C/Gas 9. Don't peel the potatoes. Just bung them into a pot of salted water, bring to the boil and simmer for around 15 minutes, until they'll take a skewer without too much resistance. They should be just about cooked, without being soft.

Drain the potatoes and arrange on a lightly oiled baking tray. Use a potato masher to squash each potato flat, until it is twice its original diameter. Brush the tops with olive oil, and scatter with sea salt, black pepper, fennel seeds and thyme sprigs.

Bake the potatoes on the top shelf of the oven for 20 to 25 minutes until crisp and golden. Serve hot.

SERVES 4
16 small, round potatoes
salt
1 tbsp extra virgin olive oil
1 tsp sea salt
freshly ground black pepper
1 tbsp fennel or caraway seeds
small handful of thyme sprigs

Beetroot rice

Whiz 3 cooked, peeled beetroot in a blender with sea salt and pepper. Heat a little butter in a fry pan and cook a finely chopped onion until soft. Add 300 g arborio (risotto) rice and stir well. Add 150 ml dry white wine, bubble it away, then add 1 litre hot chicken stock. Stir well, cover tightly and simmer gently for 15 minutes. Add the beetroot purée and cook for a few more minutes until the rice is tender. Add 2 tbsp freshly grated parmesan and serve.

Caramel salmon and lime

An unbeatable combination of Thai tastes – chilli, coriander, mint, sugar, lime juice and fish sauce – is just the thing for delicate, rich, flesh-pink salmon.

To make the sauce, dissolve the sugar in the water in a small pan and bring to the boil, stirring. Add the chilli, ginger and garlic, and let it bubble away to reduce (but not boil over) for 4 to 5 minutes until quite syrupy. Remove from the heat, and add the fish sauce and lime juice.

Cut the salmon into bite-sized pieces, about 3 cm square, and coat lightly in the caramel sauce.

Pour a jug of boiling water over the bean sprouts, then drain and set aside.

Heat the oil in a non-stick fry pan, and fry the salmon quickly until caramelised, keeping the inside pink.

Combine the salmon, mint, coriander, spring onion and bean sprouts in a bowl, and toss well. Arrange on warmed dinner plates, spoon the warm sauce over the top, and scatter with peanuts. Serve with lime quarters and plenty of rice.

SERVES 4

4 thick salmon fillets, around
    180g each
200g bean sprouts
2 tbsp vegetable oil
50g mint leaves
25g coriander leaves
1 spring onion, finely sliced
2 tbsp salted peanuts, crushed
1 lime, quartered

Sauce:
100g soft brown sugar
125ml water
1 red chilli, finely sliced
3cm knob of fresh ginger,
    finely sliced
2 garlic cloves, peeled and
    smashed
4 tbsp Thai fish sauce
4 tbsp lime juice

fast roast fish

Chinese ginger fish

A quick, easy meal for everyone who loves Cantonese-style steamed fish. The fish is best with the skin left on, as the final hot dressing will cause it to sizzle and crisp, but if you don't like the skin, you can peel it off before steaming.

SERVES 4

5cm knob of fresh ginger

1 small red chilli

3 spring onions

4 thick fresh fish fillets, with skin (eg bream, haddock, plaice, cod), around 180g each

3 tbsp soy sauce

1 tbsp sesame oil

2 tbsp Chinese rice wine, or dry sherry

1 tbsp sugar

4 tbsp groundnut or peanut oil

3 tbsp coriander leaves

Peel the ginger and cut into tiny matchsticks. Finely slice the chilli and spring onions. Gently wash the fish, pat dry and arrange on a heatproof platter that will fit into your steamer.

Mix the soy, sesame oil, rice wine and sugar together, and pour over the fish, skin-side up. Scatter the ginger, chilli and half the spring onions on top and steam for 8 to 10 minutes, until the flesh parts easily when pierced with a knife.

Transfer the fish to warmed dinner plates and strain the juices over the top. Heat the oil in a small pan until it just starts to smoke, then pour it over the fish. Scatter with the remaining spring onions and coriander, and serve with jasmine rice.

Fast roast fish

A fabulous way with fish that gives you moist, juicy, good looking fillets in 10 minutes flat. Buy the fattest, freshest fish fillets you can find.

Place a baking tray in the oven and heat the oven to 250°C/Gas 9. The tray may buckle slightly in the heat, but carry on regardless.

In the meantime, gently wash the fish and pat dry. Combine the olive oil, parsley, sea salt and pepper in a bowl, and coat each fish fillet well in the mixture. Cut the lemon into 4 thick slices.

When very hot, remove the tray from the oven and place the fish on its hot surface. Add the lemon slices, return to the top shelf of the oven and bake for 10 minutes. If you could only find thin fillets, test after 5 or 6 minutes.

Gently lift each fish fillet onto a warm dinner plate. Top with a warm slice of lemon, letting its juices run over the fish, and serve.

SERVES 4
4 thick white fish fillets (eg turbot, cod, haddock, hake), around 200g each
2 tbsp extra virgin olive oil
1 tbsp finely chopped parsley
sea salt
freshly ground pepper
1 lemon

sweet, sweet onions

Everything good starts with an onion. It gives a base of sweet complexity, a bed for all the other flavours to lie on.

know your onions

Shallots are little red or brown onions with a milder, sweeter flavour – good for salads and fast-cooked dishes. They're easier to peel if you drop them in a pot of boiling water for 3 minutes first. Torpedo-shaped banana shallots are also milder – peel, cut into rings and lightly fry. The rest you know.

the onion-balsamic trick

For rich, sweet, and fast caramelised onions, heat 1 tbsp butter and 1 tbsp olive oil in a pan. When hot, fry 2 finely sliced onions for 10 minutes, tossing. Add 2 tbsp balsamic vinegar and cook for 5 minutes until crisp, but don't burn.

fast french onion soup

Fry 6 sliced white onions in 2 tbsp butter. Add 1 tbsp flour and cook for 1 to 2 minutes, then add 1.2 litres beef or chicken stock and simmer for 20 minutes. Top with grilled slices of sourdough bread, scatter with 3 tbsp grated gruyère cheese and place under the grill until the cheese bubbles.

one for the boys

Toss 3 finely sliced red onions in 2 tbsp olive oil and place on a baking tray. Top with 4 thick sliced plum tomatoes, and scatter with salt, pepper, thyme and rosemary. Lay 8 well-pricked, thick pork or beef sausages on top. Bake at 200°C/Gas 6 for 1 hour.

don't cry, baby

To cure onion tears, place onions in the freezer for 10 minutes before cutting, or chop them in the food processor.

sweet and sour onions

Gently simmer 30 small white onions with 2 tbsp tomato purée (paste), 100 ml red wine vinegar, 2 tbsp olive oil, 2 tbsp sugar, 1 bay leaf, 250 ml dry white wine, 250 ml water and 100 g raisins for 1 hour until tender. Serve with cold meats.

the nicest way to cook onions

Heat 1 tbsp butter, 2 tbsp olive oil, sea salt, 2 bay leaves, 100 ml dry white wine and 4 finely sliced onions in a pan. Cook very slowly for 45 minutes until meltingly soft. Serve as a sauce, to a roast leg of lamb or pork. Bliss.

how to roast onions

Don't peel, just cut them crosswise through the top as if quartering, but only halfway down. Drizzle with olive oil, scatter with thyme sprigs and bake at 180°C/Gas 4 for 1 hour for soft, sweet, irresistible onions.

the 15 minute dinner

Fry 2 chopped onions in a little butter and oil for 5 minutes. Add some chopped, leftover cooked ham, chicken or vegetables, and fry for 5 minutes. Stir in 3 eggs, salt, pepper and a pinch of cayenne, and cook until golden.

everyone loves onion rings

For crisp onion rings, submerge thickly sliced white onion rings in icy cold water for 1 hour. Drain and pat dry with paper towel, toss in flour and deep-fry. Serve with grilled fish, sausages, steaks and char-grilled veg.

simple
entertaining

Chilli orange duck

Here is a nice twist on duck à l'orange – aromatic, crisp-skinned duck in a sticky, sweet and spicy citrus syrup that glows on the plate.

Scrub the oranges well. Cut the rind from 2 oranges, using a sharp knife, and trim off most of the pith. Cut the rind into short, thin strips. Squeeze the juice from the oranges – you need 250 ml.

Combine the orange rind and juice, sugar, ginger, chilli, star anise, cinnamon sticks, sweet chilli sauce, fish sauce, vinegar and red wine in a saucepan and bring to the boil, stirring. Boil for around 10 minutes, stirring occasionally, until lightly syrupy.

Prick the duck skin well, and heat the oil in a non-stick fry pan. Add the duck breasts and sear, skin-side down, for 8 minutes until browned, then turn and cook for another 8 minutes. Rest for 5 minutes before serving.

Cut the spring onions into finger lengths, then into strips. Slice the duck thickly, arrange on warmed plates and scatter with spring onion shreds. Spoon the sauce over the top, with the spices – for atmosphere, not for eating. Serve with rice or noodles.

SERVES 4

2–3 oranges

100 g sugar

1 tbsp grated fresh ginger

1 small red chilli, finely sliced

2 star anise

2 cinnamon sticks

1 tbsp sweet chilli sauce

1 tbsp Thai fish sauce

1 tbsp rice wine vinegar, or
   other wine vinegar

2 tbsp red wine or port

4 duck breasts, around
   200 g each

1 tbsp vegetable oil

2 spring onions, trimmed

Pancetta chicken

Wash and pat dry 8 large, boned chicken thighs. Mix
1 tbsp grated lemon rind with 2 crushed garlic cloves,
2 tbsp chopped parsley, sea salt and pepper, and rub
into the inside of each thigh. Roll up and wrap in slices
of pancetta or thin bacon. Bake at 180°C/Gas 4 for
45 minutes or until tender. Serve on buttered sweetcorn.

steak with mushrooms

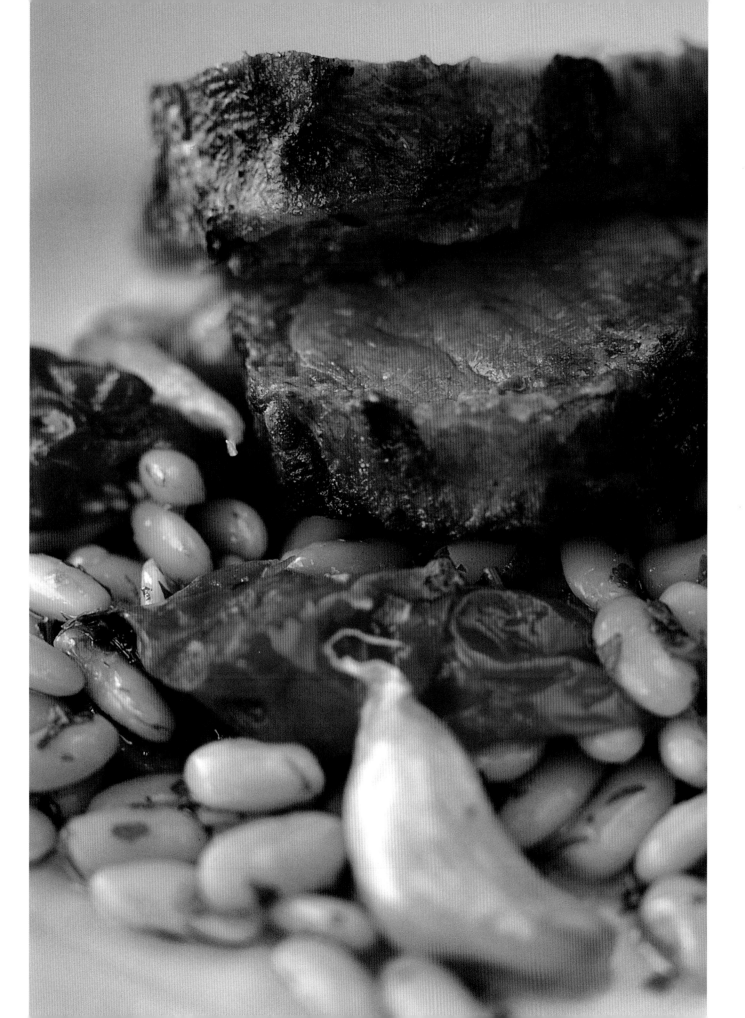

Steak with mushrooms

A rich and creamy mushroom sauce smothers pan-seared steaks in a sort of beef stroganoff for the 21st century.

Cut the onion in half and slice finely. Wipe the mushrooms, discard the stalks and slice finely.

Melt the butter with the olive oil in a non-stick fry pan, and gently cook the onion for 5 minutes. Add the mushrooms and cook for 5 minutes. Add white wine, sea salt, pepper and paprika, and bring to the boil, stirring. Reduce the heat and simmer for 5 minutes.

Heat a cast-iron grill pan or another heavy non-stick fry pan. Brush the steaks with a little olive oil and cook on one side, without moving, for 2 minutes. Season, turn, and cook for 2 to 3 minutes for medium rare. Season again, and leave to rest in a warm place.

Add the sour cream, mustard, tomato purée and most of the parsley to the mushrooms and cook, stirring, for 5 minutes. Place the steaks on warmed plates, spoon the mushroom sauce on top and scatter with the remaining chopped parsley.

SERVES 4

1 onion, peeled

500g mushrooms

1 tbsp butter

1 tbsp olive oil

125ml white wine

sea salt

freshly ground black pepper

1 tsp sweet paprika

4 rump steaks, around 200g
   each, and 2.5cm thick

3 tbsp sour cream or crème
   fraîche

1 tsp Dijon mustard

1 tbsp tomato purée (paste)

1 tbsp finely chopped parsley

Grilled lamb and beans

The best way to get great looking lamb chops is to buy a well-trimmed rack of lamb and divide it into 4 double chops.

Heat the oven to 180°C/Gas 4. Toss the cherry tomatoes and garlic cloves in 1 tbsp olive oil in a small roasting pan, and bake for 30 minutes.

Heat a cast-iron grill pan, or the grill, until hot. Cut the rack of lamb into 4 double chops, and swipe them in the hot oil of the roasting tomatoes. Grill, skin-side down for 3 minutes, then for around 2 to 3 minutes on either side for medium rare, depending on size.

Drain and rinse the canned beans. Heat them gently with the remaining 2 tbsp extra virgin olive oil, sea salt, black pepper and chopped parsley. Divide between warmed plates.

Cut each chop in two or leave whole if you prefer, and arrange on the beans. Quickly toss the roasted tomatoes and garlic with the basil and spoon around the chops. Squeeze out the soft garlic from the skins to eat with the lamb.

SERVES 4

200 g cherry tomatoes

4 garlic cloves, lightly smashed

3 tbsp extra virgin olive oil

1 x 8-chop rack of lamb (well trimmed)

400 g canned white beans (cannellini or flageolet)

sea salt

freshly ground black pepper

2 tbsp finely chopped parsley

handful of basil leaves

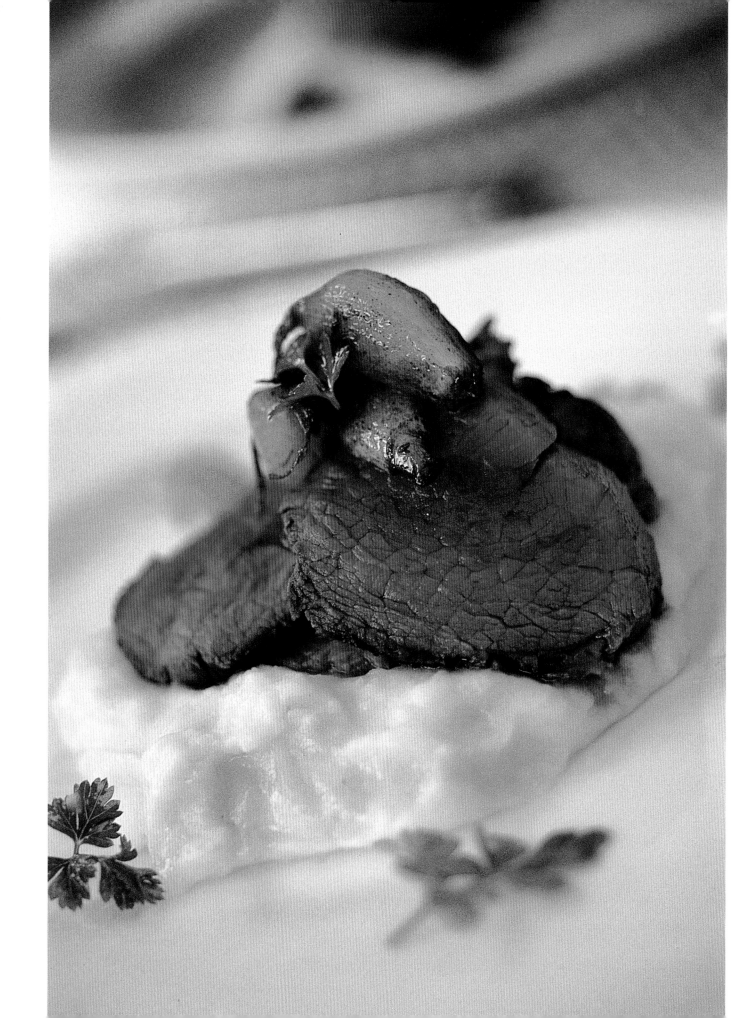

Beef with shallots

My friends tell me that every time they cook this, their guests say it's just like eating in a restaurant. It is better than that, though. Restaurants don't give you second helpings of mash.

Cook the unpeeled shallots in simmering water for 5 minutes, then drain and peel.

Heat the grill, or a cast-iron grill pan or fry pan, until hot. Rub the beef with 1 tbsp olive oil, sea salt and pepper. Grill or pan-sear the beef on all sides until well marked, but still rare inside, around 12 minutes. Remove from the heat and allow to rest for 10 minutes.

In the meantime, cook the potatoes in a pan of simmering salted water until tender.

Heat the remaining 1 tbsp olive oil in a fry pan, and fry the shallots for about 10 minutes until golden. Add the balsamic vinegar, thyme and rosemary sprigs, and cook gently, stirring as the shallots colour and caramelise.

Gently heat the milk with the smashed garlic until hot. Drain the potatoes and mash well, then beat in the milk, discarding the garlic.

Discard the string, slice the beef into 1cm thick slices and season with salt and pepper. Spoon the mash onto warmed plates and arrange the beef on top with the caramelised shallots. Scatter with parsley or chervil to serve.

SERVES 4

20 small brown shallots
600g rolled fillet of beef, tied with string
2 tbsp extra virgin olive oil
sea salt
freshly ground black pepper
600g red-skinned potatoes, peeled
2 tbsp balsamic vinegar
few thyme and rosemary sprigs
125ml milk
2 garlic cloves, peeled and smashed
parsley or chervil sprigs, to serve

Salmon in cabbage

An elegant way to serve an elegant fish for a dinner party or special meal. Easy, too, because you can package up the salmon beforehand, ready for steaming when you want to eat.

Peel off and discard the outer leaves of the cabbage, then carefully peel off 4 good, bright coloured leaves. Drop them into a pot of simmering, salted water for 3 minutes, then drain and rinse under cold water. Shave off any inner ribs on the blanched leaves.

Trim the salmon fillets into neat squares, and remove any pin bones. Spread out a sheet of cling film on a work surface and lay a blanched cabbage leaf on top. Place a salmon fillet in the middle, season well, and gently wrap the leaf around it to make a parcel. Wrap the parcel tightly in the cling film. Repeat to make the remaining parcels, and chill.

SERVES 4

1 firm Savoy cabbage

4 salmon fillets, around 180g
    each, and 3cm thick

sea salt

freshly ground black pepper

2 tomatoes

2 tbsp extra virgin olive oil

1 tbsp tiny capers, rinsed

1 lemon, quartered

Cut the tomatoes in half, and squeeze out and discard the seeds and juice. Finely chop the flesh.

Fill the base of your steamer with water and bring to the boil. Carefully remove the cling film from the cabbage parcels, place them in the steamer, cover tightly and cook for 8 to 10 minutes.

Gently warm the chopped tomatoes, extra virgin olive oil and capers in a pan. Place the cabbage parcels on warmed plates and spoon the tomato salsa over and around them. Serve with lemon wedges and small boiled potatoes.

Teriyaki salmon

Japan's brilliant way with steak also suits the healthy richness of salmon. Serve on a mangetout (snow pea) salad for a really crisp, fresh bite.

To make the teriyaki sauce, combine the sugar, sake, mirin and soy sauce in a bowl, and set aside.

Wash and dry the mangetout, trim if necessary, then finely slice lengthwise into matchsticks, using the tip of a sharp knife. Mix the rice wine vinegar and sesame oil together in a bowl, add the mangetout and toss until coated.

Remove any pin bones from the salmon fillets and pat dry with paper towel. Heat the vegetable oil in a heavy non-stick fry pan. Cook the fillets, skin-side down, for around 2 minutes or until the skin is crisp and you can see the flesh gradually changing colour.

Turn the fillets and add most of the teriyaki sauce to the pan. Allow the sauce to bubble up around the salmon as you cook the other side for about 3 minutes, leaving the middle pink. (Don't allow to boil dry, or the sugar will burn.)

Divide the mangetout between plates and arrange the salmon fillets on top. Quickly heat the remaining teriyaki sauce and spoon it over the salmon to serve.

SERVES 4
250g mangetout (snow peas)
1 tbsp rice wine vinegar, or white wine vinegar
2 tsp sesame oil
4 salmon fillets with skin, around 180g each
1 tbsp vegetable oil

Teriyaki sauce:
1 tbsp sugar
3 tbsp sake (Japanese rice wine)
2 tbsp mirin (sweet rice wine), or sweet sherry
3 tbsp soy sauce

Swordfish with courgettes

Seared swordfish gets dressed up with courgettes (zucchini) and a lemony, herby Mediterranean dressing, known as salmoriglio. This is a great way to serve fresh tuna steaks too.

Trim the courgettes, discarding the ends, then grate coarsely. Heat 2 tbsp olive oil in a non-stick fry pan and add the courgettes with sea salt and black pepper. Toss well over a medium heat for 2 to 3 minutes until softened.

Heat 1 tbsp olive oil in a non-stick fry pan. When hot, season the swordfish well and sear on one side until quite golden, about 3 minutes. Turn and cook the other side for another 2 minutes, depending on the thickness.

To make the dressing, whisk the lemon juice, olive oil and sea salt in a bowl, and stir in the parsley, oregano and capers.

Arrange the swordfish on a bed of courgettes and top with a caper berry or a few extra capers. Serve the dressing in a bowl, to be spooned on top.

SERVES 4

4 medium courgettes
    (zucchini)
3 tbsp olive oil
sea salt
freshly ground black pepper
6 swordfish steaks, around
    180g each
4 caper berries, or a few
    extra capers

Salmoriglio dressing:
2 tbsp lemon juice
6 tbsp extra virgin olive oil
1/2 tsp sea salt
2 tbsp parsley leaves
2 tsp oregano leaves
2 tbsp capers, rinsed

Chilli basil mussels

Enticing, invigorating, exciting and exotic, this is a great dish of Thai flavours for mussel lovers.

Scrub the mussels well, pulling out the little beards, and discard any that do not close when sharply tapped. Pick the basil and mint leaves from their stems.

Heat the oil in a wok, and stir-fry the garlic and ginger for just 30 seconds. Carefully add the wine and boil for 30 seconds, then add the fish sauce, chillies and half the mussels. Cover and steam for 1 minute, shake the pan, then remove the opened mussels. Do this another two or three times, then discard any mussels that don't open. Repeat with remaining mussels.

Bring the broth to the boil, and add the chilli sauce and most of the basil and mint leaves, stirring. Return the mussels to the pan, briefly tossing well over high heat. Scatter with the remaining basil and mint to serve.

SERVES 4
2kg mussels
bunch of basil
bunch of mint
2 tbsp vegetable oil
3 garlic cloves, peeled and smashed
1 tbsp finely chopped fresh ginger
125ml dry white wine
2 tbsp Thai fish sauce
2 red chillies, finely chopped
3 tbsp sweet, seedy Thai chilli sauce

Roast tamari veg

Tamari is a Japanese wheat-free soy sauce with a deeper, more complex flavour than your standard soy. Use normal soy if you don't have it.

Heat the oven to 200°C/Gas 6. Cut the pumpkin into thinnish wedges, cut off the skin, and discard the seeds. Wash the carrots, peel and trim the tops neatly. Peel the parsnips and cut lengthwise into quarters. Peel and halve the beetroot.

Combine the tamari, olive oil, sea salt and pepper in a big bowl, add the vegetables and toss until well coated. Tip into a baking tray and bake for 45 minutes to 1 hour until tender and nicely browned.

To make the dressing, whisk the rice wine vinegar, fish sauce, olive oil and sugar together in a bowl. Drizzle over the vegetables, jumble everything up a bit and pile high on warmed serving plates. Scatter with coriander to serve.

SERVES 4

500g pumpkin

2 bunches of baby carrots

4 parsnips

4 fresh beetroot

2 tbsp tamari, or soy sauce

2 tbsp extra virgin olive oil

$\frac{1}{2}$ tsp sea salt

$\frac{1}{2}$ tsp freshly ground black pepper

handful of coriander leaves

Dressing:

2 tbsp rice wine vinegar, or white wine vinegar

1 tbsp Thai fish sauce

3 tbsp extra virgin olive oil

1 tbsp sugar

simple suppers

Penne with tuna

Cook little cubes of potato in the same pot as the pasta, and they'll be soft and lush by the time they hit the tuna and caper sauce. If you need an extra flavour hit, add a finely chopped red chilli with the olives.

Peel the potatoes and chop into 1 cm cubes. Bring a large pot of salted water to the boil, add the pasta and potatoes and cook together until tender, around 10 minutes depending on the pasta.

Drain the tuna, reserving the oil. Heat the olive oil in a pan, and add the tuna, olives and capers. Toss well until everything is hot.

Drain the cooked pasta and potatoes and add to the sauce with most of the tuna oil. Add the basil or rocket leaves with sea salt and pepper, and toss well over the heat until wilted.

SERVES 4

4 medium potatoes

500g penne or rigatoni

300g canned tuna in olive oil

1 tbsp olive oil

20 small black olives

2 tbsp salted capers, rinsed

small bunch of basil, or 100g
   baby rocket leaves

sea salt

freshly ground black pepper

Orecchiette with rocket

Finely slice 2 red chillies and 2 garlic cloves. Gently heat with 2 tbsp extra virgin olive oil in a big fry pan, stirring. Add 300 g rocket leaves and toss until wilted, then add 450 g cooked, drained orecchiette or similar pasta. Toss well and scatter with grated parmesan.

Baked spaghetti

The good thing about this supper is that you can cook everything beforehand and put it together, then just bake in the oven when you're ready to eat.

Finely chop the onion. Heat the olive oil in a large fry pan and cook the onion for 10 minutes. Add the garlic and minced meat and stir over high heat until it browns. Sprinkle with flour and cook, stirring, for 3 minutes.

Add the white wine and boil for 1 minute, then add the tomatoes, tomato purée, stock, sea salt, pepper, nutmeg and rosemary sprigs. Partially cover and cook gently for 45 minutes.

Heat the oven to 180°C/Gas 4. Cook the pasta in plenty of boiling salted water until tender but firm. Drain well, then toss with the sauce. Scatter with parmesan, pile into a lightly oiled serving dish and bake for 30 minutes until crisp on top.

SERVES 4

1 onion, peeled

2 tbsp olive oil

2 garlic cloves, peeled and crushed

500g minced pork, veal or beef

1 tbsp plain flour

125ml white wine

800g canned chopped tomatoes

1 tbsp tomato purée (paste)

250ml chicken stock or water

sea salt

freshly ground black pepper

1/2 tsp freshly grated nutmeg

few rosemary or oregano sprigs

500g spaghetti

2 tbsp freshly grated parmesan

chilli soy tofu

Chilli soy tofu

Even if you don't like tofu, you'll like this tofu. Serve with rice for a light, simple supper for two, or team it with the Asian omelette on page 143, or stir-fry duck noodles opposite, for a more substantial supper for four.

Fill the base of your steamer with water and bring to the boil.

Drain the tofu and place it on a heatproof plate that will fit inside the steamer. Steam the tofu for 20 minutes, then drain off excess water and carefully transfer to a serving plate.

Finely slice the red chilli. Trim and finely slice the spring onions.

Heat the soy sauce, sesame oil and oyster sauce together in a small pan until hot. Pour the mixture over the tofu, scatter with red chilli, spring onion and coriander leaves, and serve.

SERVES 2

500g pack fresh tofu

1 small red chilli

2 spring onions

3 tbsp soy sauce

2 tsp sesame oil

1 tsp oyster sauce

2 tbsp coriander leaves

Stir-fry duck noodles

Oiled egg noodles, also known as Hokkien or stir-fry noodles, look like fat golden spaghetti. Oriental food stores and larger supermarkets sell them. Pick up barbecued roast duck from Chinatown, or use leftover duck or barbecued chicken.

Remove the meat from the duck and finely slice it, discarding the bones. Finely chop the spring onions, celery and chilli.

Heat a wok or fry pan, add the oil and heat. Add the ginger and garlic and cook until golden to flavour the oil, then remove and discard. Add the celery, chilli and half the spring onions and stir-fry for 2 minutes. Add the duck and stir-fry for 1 minute.

Put the noodles in a heatproof bowl, cover with boiling water, then drain immediately. Add to the wok and toss well over high heat.

Add the bean sprouts, toss, then add the rice wine. Add the hoi sin, oyster and soy sauces, and toss well. Scatter with the remaining spring onions and serve.

SERVES 4

½ roast duck (eg Chinese barbecued roast duck)

3 spring onions

2 celery stalks

1 small red chilli

2 tbsp vegetable oil

1 slice fresh ginger

1 garlic clove, peeled and smashed

400g fresh oiled egg noodles

200g bean sprouts, rinsed

1 tbsp Chinese rice wine, or dry sherry

1 tbsp hoi sin sauce

2 tbsp oyster sauce

2 tbsp soy sauce

Asian omelette

This works well with leftover roast pork, or barbecued Chinese char sieu pork from Chinatown. It is also delicious with cooked prawns or crabmeat instead of the meat.

Finely slice the roast pork. Rinse the bean sprouts in boiling water and drain. Wash the watercress, and shake dry.

To make one omelette, crack 2 eggs into a small bowl, and lightly beat in 1 tbsp rice wine, salt, pepper and $\frac{1}{2}$ tsp sesame oil.

Heat 1 tbsp vegetable oil in a hot wok over high heat, swirling it around to coat the entire surface. Pour in the beaten eggs and quickly swirl to form an even omelette. Cook for 2 to 3 minutes until the egg is firm, then lower the heat.

Arrange some roast pork in the centre, top with bean sprouts and watercress, and cook gently for a further 2 or 3 minutes.

Loosen the edges with a knife, then gently slide the omelette onto a warm plate, folding it over. Keep it warm while you make three more omelettes. Drizzle with oyster sauce to serve.

SERVES 4
450g boneless roast or
barbecued pork
400g bean sprouts
200g watercress
8 large free-range eggs
4 tbsp Chinese rice wine,
or dry sherry
sea salt
freshly ground black pepper
2 tsp sesame oil
4 tbsp vegetable oil
4 tbsp oyster or hoi sin sauce

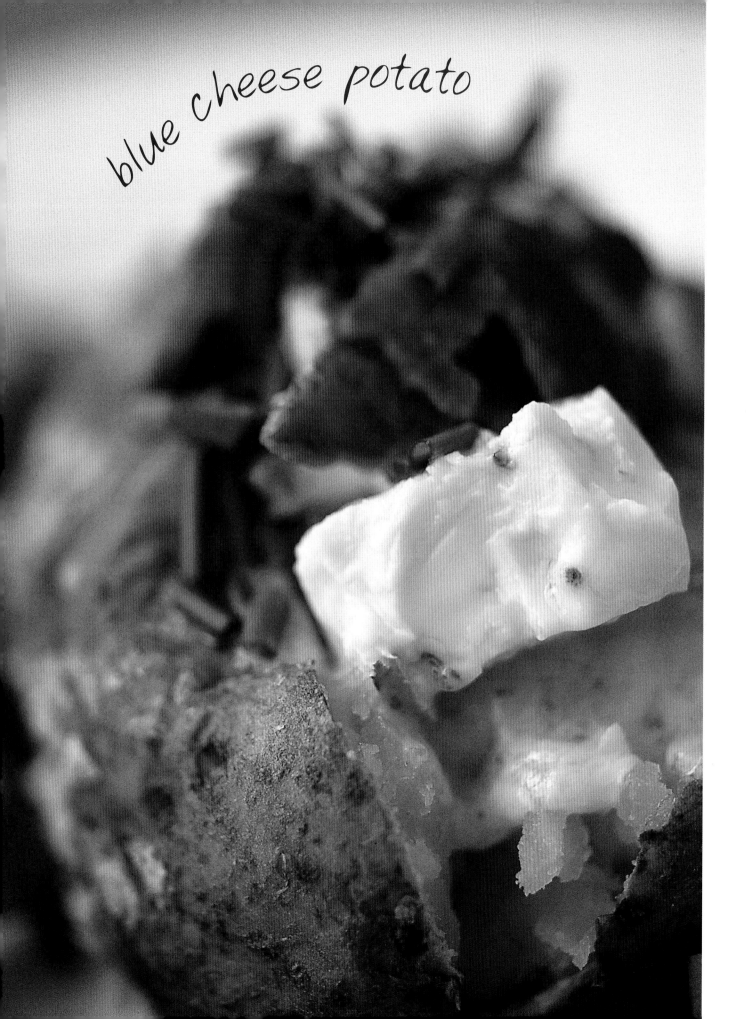

blue cheese potato

Onions with cheese

Everyone who loves baked onions calls this a great supper. Those who quite like them call it a great side dish for lamb, chicken or steak.

Heat the oven to 180°C/Gas 4. Peel the onions and arrange them in a lightly oiled baking tray so that they fit snugly side by side.

Drizzle with the olive oil and bake for 1 hour until soft. Remove from the oven, and turn the heat to 220°C/Gas 7.

Combine the grated parmesan, nutmeg, sea salt, black pepper and cream in a jug or bowl, stirring well.

Pour the cream over the baked onions, and sprinkle with paprika. Return the dish to the oven for about 15 minutes until the cheese sauce is golden brown and bubbling. Let stand for a minute or two before serving.

SERVES 4

8 medium white onions

2 tbsp olive oil

4 tbsp freshly grated parmesan

pinch of freshly grated nutmeg

sea salt

freshly ground black pepper

250 ml single or whipping
 cream

1/2 tsp smoked paprika

Blue cheese potato

Put the spuds in the oven just before you go out for a quick drink or an evening meeting, return an hour or so later and supper is almost done.

Heat the oven to 200°C/Gas 6. Scrub the potatoes well and dry thoroughly. Prick lightly, coat in olive oil, and roll in salt and pepper.

Place the potatoes on the rack in the centre of the oven and bake for $1^1/_2$ to 2 hours, until soft to the touch. (If you can hear them softly whistle, they're perfect.)

Fry the bacon in a non-stick fry pan until crisp, drain well on paper towel, and chop or crumble into shards.

Cut a cross in the top of each potato, and push in at the edges to expose the inside. Pile the sour cream and blue cheese on top, scatter with bacon and chives, and serve before it all melts.

SERVES 4
4 large baking potatoes
(eg King Edward), around
250g each
1 tbsp olive oil
1 tsp sea salt
freshly ground black pepper
4 rashers streaky bacon
150g sour cream or
crème fraîche
150g gorgonzola or Roquefort,
crumbled
2 tbsp finely chopped chives
or parsley

Hash browns with bacon rolls

Plum tomatoes and honeyed bacon roast themselves, while you grate the potatoes and onion, and fry them into sweet-smelling, herb-strewn hash browns.

Heat the oven to 200°C/Gas 6. Cut the tomatoes in half lengthwise, season with sea salt and pepper, and arrange on a baking tray. Roll the bacon rashers into tight rolls and place on the same tray. Drizzle bacon rolls with honey and bake for 20 minutes, or until the tomatoes are soft and the bacon is crisp.

Peel the potatoes and onion, coarsely grate them, then wrap in a clean cloth and squeeze out excess liquid. Place in a bowl, add the beaten egg, flour, chopped herbs, 1 tsp sea salt and the olive oil, and stir well.

Heat 1 tbsp vegetable oil in a fry pan until hot, then add 2 heaped tablespoons of the potato mixture. Squash them flat and fry gently on both sides until golden brown. Keep them warm in the oven while you cook the remaining hash browns, adding a little extra oil to the pan each time.

Serve the hash browns topped with the roasted tomato halves, crisp bacon rolls and rosemary.

SERVES 4

4 plum tomatoes

sea salt

freshly ground black pepper

8 thin rashers rindless bacon,
   halved if large

1 tsp runny honey

6 medium potatoes

1 small onion

1 large free-range egg, beaten

1 tbsp plain flour

2 tbsp chopped herbs
   (eg thyme, rosemary, chives)

1 tbsp olive oil

3 tbsp vegetable oil

rosemary sprigs, to serve

herby Potatoes, crisp honeyed bacon

warm, glowing spices

Sweet cinnamon, bitter saffron, nutty coriander, and floral nutmeg

teach us to cook with all of our senses, adding warmth and perfume

by the spoonful.

toast before use

There is nothing wrong with buying ground or powdered spices, but you will get more flavour if you buy whole spices and lightly toast them in a dry fry pan as you need them. Grind in an electric coffee grinder or pulverise with a pestle and mortar.

cinnamon coconut rice

Place 300 g rinsed jasmine rice in a pan with 300 ml coconut milk, 300 ml water, salt, 2 cinnamon sticks and 2 star anise, and bring to the boil. Cover tightly and simmer very gently, undisturbed, for 15 minutes. Rest for 10 minutes, then fluff up with a fork and serve with curry.

cinnamon toast

Shake 2 tbsp granulated sugar with 1–2 tsp ground cinnamon in a jar. Grill the bread on one side, turn, butter the untoasted side, sprinkle with cinnamon sugar and lightly grill until melted.

sticky cardamom toffee syrup

Gently heat 150 g soft brown sugar, 25 ml cream, 1 split vanilla pod, 2 tbsp butter and 2 crushed cardamom pods until the sugar dissolves, then simmer for 5 minutes. Strain and serve over steamed puds, cakes and poached pears.

sweet, mulled wine

Combine 750 ml light red wine and 250 ml Muscat or port with a split vanilla pod, 2 cinnamon sticks, 8 cloves, 2 bay leaves and the rind of half an orange. Cover and leave overnight to infuse. Heat gently, add 200 g sugar, stirring, and serve warm.

clever with cloves

Strong little spikes of punchy flavour, cloves are the dried flower buds of an evergreen tree native to Indonesia. Stick them in an onion when cooking savoury dishes, or an orange for sweet dishes, so you can take them out easily at the end.

grind your own nutmeg

Whole nutmeg is far superior to ready ground. Freshly grate or grind for cakes, soups, custards, quiches and rice pud.

the joy of red-cooking

Make a brilliant Chinese braise with 250 ml soy sauce, 200 ml chicken stock, 2 tbsp rice wine or dry sherry, 1 tsp sesame oil, some fresh ginger and garlic, 1 tbsp sugar and 3 star anise, and simmer for 10 minutes. Use it to poach Chinese mushrooms, chicken, fish or pork, to serve with rice.

dip into Egyptian dukkah

In a hot, dry pan, toast 100 g sesame seeds, 100 g blanched almonds, 50 g coriander seeds and 10 g cumin seeds until fragrant, stirring. Cool, then coarsely grind with 1 tsp sea salt and ½ tsp pepper. Serve with warm Turkish bread and olive oil.

a great rice pulao

Fry 1 chopped onion in 1 tbsp oil. Add 1 tsp each cumin seeds and brown mustard seeds, 2 crushed cardamom pods, 1 bay leaf, 1 cinnamon stick, salt, pepper and ½ tsp each of ground cumin, coriander and turmeric. Add 300 g rinsed rice and 600 ml boiling water, cover and simmer very gently for 15 minutes.

simple sweets

Rhubarb sponge pud

The good thing about this pudding is that the rhubarb cooks itself under the golden sponge topping.

Heat the oven to 180°C/Gas 4. Cream the butter and sugar together in a bowl until light. Add the eggs, one at a time, beating well. Sift the flour into the bowl, folding it through quickly with a large metal spoon or spatula.

Cut the rhubarb stalks into 2 cm lengths, discarding any leaves. Arrange in a tumbled fashion in a buttered 1 litre pie or baking dish and scatter with the 80 g caster sugar.

Spoon the mixture on top of the fruit and bake for 50 to 60 minutes until the topping is a golden sponge cake and the rhubarb is tender. (If the topping appears to brown too quickly in the oven, cover lightly with foil.) Serve with rich cream.

SERVES 4

Sponge topping:

100 g butter, soft

100 g caster sugar

2 large free-range eggs

100 g self-raising flour, sifted

Fruit filling:

500 g ripe rhubarb stalks

80 g caster sugar

Sugar plums

Brush 8 ripe
plums with beaten
egg white, then roll
in 3 tbsp white sugar to
coat well. Bake on a foil-lined tray
at 200°C/Gas 6 for 15 minutes until
soft. Serve with mascarpone,
or the caramel yoghurt on
page 175.

Banana ice-cream

All the fun of banana ice-cream, without the sugar, eggs or cream. Peel 8 firm ripe bananas, wrap in cling film and freeze overnight. Soften for 20 minutes, then roughly chop and whiz until thick and creamy. Eat now, or refreeze, in which case soften for 20 minutes before you slice or scoop.

Baked banana split

Bake 4 unpeeled bananas at 180°C/Gas 4
for 30 minutes until the skin is black. Finely chop
100g dark, bitter chocolate and 2 tbsp walnuts. Gently slit
the skin and peel back the top part. Scatter the split with
chocolate and nuts, then serve with ice-cream.

Little lemon pots

Tangy little lemon custards can be baked ahead and served at room temperature, making them perfect for entertaining. You'll need 2 to 3 lemons, depending on their size. Serve with the coconut macaroons on page 182, for crunch.

Heat the oven to 160°C/Gas 3. Whisk the eggs and sugar in a bowl until well mixed. Stir in the lemon rind and juice, and lightly whisk in the cream.

Skim off and discard any froth, then strain the custard into six 100 ml ovenproof pots or Chinese ovenproof white tea cups.

Stand in a shallow baking tin, and fill the tin with hot water to come halfway up the sides of the pots. Bake for 20 to 25 minutes or until the custards have set, with just a tiny wobble on the surface. Remove from the baking tin.

Serve either warm or at room temperature, dusted with icing sugar.

SERVES 6

6 large free-range eggs

175 g caster sugar

2 tsp grated lemon rind

125 ml lemon juice

150 ml single or whipping cream

icing sugar for dusting

blood orange jelly

Blood orange jelly

As wobbly as a runaway bride, this do-ahead jelly fills the mouth with its powerful tang. You'll need 3 to 4 blood oranges, depending on their size.

Put a few spoonfuls of the measured water in a small heatproof bowl and sprinkle with the powdered gelatine. Leave to soften for 5 minutes, then warm gently over a pan of hot water for about 5 minutes until dissolved.

Dissolve the sugar in the remaining water in a small pan, stirring, then bring to the boil. Remove from heat, add the blood orange juice and whisk in the dissolved gelatine.

SERVES 4

200ml water

15g powdered gelatine

200g sugar

250ml blood orange juice

To serve:

4 slices blood orange

2 tbsp blood orange juice

Rinse four 100ml moulds with cold water, and shake dry. Fill with the orange liquid, allow to cool, then refrigerate for several hours until set.

To serve, dip the base of each mould very briefly in hot water, run a knife around the edge to loosen the jelly and turn out onto a serving plate. Top each jelly with an orange slice and drizzle with a little extra juice to serve.

Roast vanilla peaches

One of the great quandaries of summer is whether to just scoff all the glorious fruit as it comes to hand, or whether to cook it. Here's one good, very simple and deliciously fragrant reason to cook it.

Heat the oven to 200°C/Gas 6. Combine the white wine, sugar, cinnamon sticks and vanilla pod in a small saucepan. Heat, stirring, until the sugar dissolves, then boil for 1 minute.

Place the peaches in a small, shallow baking tin and pour in the wine mixture. Bake in the centre of the oven for 30 to 40 minutes or until the skins start to split, and the peaches look all toasty and flushed. Strain the juices into a jug.

Serve the peaches warm or at room temperature, drizzled with their cooking juices. If you have any summer berries around, warm them gently in the poaching liquid and serve with the peaches.

SERVES 4 OR 8
750 ml dry white wine
200 g caster sugar
2 cinnamon sticks
1 vanilla pod, split lengthwise
8 firm, ripe peaches
handful of summer berries
(optional)

Little peach tarts

I don't believe these need either cream or ice-cream, but feel free to disagree.

Heat the oven to 200°C/Gas 6. To peel the peaches, dunk them in a pot of boiling water for 5 seconds and the skins will peel off easily. Halve each peach, cutting around the side of the stone.

Roll out the pastry on a lightly floured surface and cut out eight circles, 10 cm in diameter. Place on lightly oiled baking sheets and brush with beaten egg.

Place a peach half, cut-side down, on top of each pastry round. Drizzle the peaches with a little honey, and dot with butter. Bake for around 20 minutes until the peaches are soft and the pastry is risen and lightly scorched.

Using a warm spoon, drizzle a little more honey over each peach – this will glaze it beautifully. Serve warm or at room temperature.

SERVES 4 OR 8

4 large firm, ripe peaches

500 g packet ready-rolled puff
  pastry

1 egg, beaten

2 tbsp runny honey

1 tbsp butter, softened

1 extra tbsp runny honey,
  to serve

Moroccan rice pud

A creamy, plump rice pudding, scented with cinnamon and fragrant orange flower water – cooked in the pot.

Combine the rice, salt, milk, water and cinnamon stick in a heavy-based saucepan and bring to the boil, stirring constantly to prevent the rice sticking.

Reduce the heat and simmer at a gentle bubble, stirring from time to time, for 15 to 20 minutes or until the rice is plump, but the texture is still slightly runny.

Remove the cinnamon stick. Add the butter, sugar and orange flower water, and stir until dissolved.

Spoon the rice into warmed pudding bowls and serve warm or at room temperature, dusted with cinnamon.

SERVES 4

180 g arborio (risotto) rice

pinch of salt

600 ml milk

150 ml water

1 cinnamon stick

1 tsp butter

3 tbsp caster sugar

2 tbsp orange flower water, or rosewater

1 tsp ground cinnamon or nutmeg for dusting

Gooey chocolate pud

An oozy, boozy chocolate pudding with a soft, gooey – almost liquid – centre.

Heat the oven to 190°C/Gas 5. Butter four 150 ml heatproof soufflé dishes or ramekins and place on a baking tray. Chop the chocolate roughly and melt in a heatproof bowl set over a pot of gently simmering water. Remove from the heat, stir well and allow to cool slightly.

Beat in the vanilla essence, brandy and sugar. Beat in the egg yolks, one by one, and then the flour. The mixture will be fairly stiff.

Whisk or beat the egg whites until stiff and peaky, then gently fold them into the chocolate mixture. Pour into the dishes and bake for 10 to 12 minutes until puffed and well risen. The puddings should still be gooey inside.

SERVES 4

1 tsp butter

150g dark, bitter chocolate

½ tsp vanilla essence

1 tbsp brandy, rum or whisky

85g caster sugar

4 large free-range eggs, separated

1 tbsp plain flour, sifted

simple treats

Little chocolate cakes

If you can melt butter, you can make these cakes. Be brave and pull them out of the oven while they're still squidgy in the middle, for a dense, fudgy, heavenly treat.

Heat the oven to 180°C/Gas 4. Roughly chop the chocolate. Fit a heatproof bowl over a saucepan of simmering water, and combine the chocolate, sugar and butter in the bowl. Stir as it melts into a smooth, glossy sauce. Remove from heat and cool for 5 minutes.

Add the ground almonds and stir well. Beat in the egg yolks, one by one, until well mixed.

MAKES 12

200g dark, bitter chocolate

100g caster sugar

120g butter

100g ground almonds

4 eggs, separated

icing sugar for dusting

Place the egg whites in a large dry bowl and beat until stiff and peaky. Stir a large spoonful of egg white into the chocolate mixture to lighten it, then gently fold in the remaining egg white.

Spoon the mixture into lightly buttered large muffin moulds, or a 12-hole muffin tray lined with doubled muffin paper cases, and bake for 25 to 30 minutes.

Leave to cool for 10 minutes before removing from the moulds. Serve at room temperature, dusted with icing sugar, or store in an airtight tin for up to 3 days.

Caramel yoghurt

How easy is this? Combine rich Greek yoghurt with whipped cream, sprinkle with brown sugar, place in the fridge and you have a luscious caramel-topped creamy treat an hour later.

Whip the cream in a bowl until peaky. Lightly fold in the Greek yoghurt, using a spatula or large spoon, then pour into a wide, shallow bowl.

Scatter the soft brown sugar evenly over the surface. Cover and chill for 1 hour, until the sugar melts to form a caramel syrup.

When ready to serve, swirl the caramel sauce through the yoghurt. Serve with poached fruits, pies and tarts, chocolate cake, or as you would any rich cream.

SERVES 4
200 ml whipping cream
200 g thick Greek yoghurt
3 tbsp soft dark brown sugar

Baby fruit cakes

These soft, fruity little cakes are so easy to make, it's almost spooky. Don't go on a picnic without them.

Heat the oven to 180°C/Gas 4. Combine the butter, sultanas, currants, sugar, mixed spice, cinnamon, ginger, bicarbonate of soda and water in a saucepan. Bring to the boil, stirring, then remove from the heat and allow to cool.

Add the eggs and beat well. Sift the two flours together, add to the mixture, and beat thoroughly.

Pour into lightly buttered or oiled muffin tin moulds or a muffin tray lined with muffin paper cases. Bake for 30 minutes, or until a skewer inserted into the centre comes out clean.

Allow to cool before removing from the moulds. Store in an airtight container for up to 3 days.

MAKES 16

150g butter

300g sultanas

300g currants

180g soft brown sugar

1 tsp ground mixed spice

1 tsp ground cinnamon

1 tsp ground ginger

1 tsp bicarbonate of soda

250ml water

2 eggs, well beaten

150g plain flour

150g self-raising flour

my friend the friand

anytime shortbread

My friend the friand

The friand is a truly awesome small, moist, dense, rich, almondy cake. It's very, very French, and very, very chic.

Heat the oven to 200°C/Gas 6. Melt the butter and allow to cool, then use 1 tbsp to coat 10 muffin tin moulds or individual oval baking moulds measuring 5 x 10 cm.

Sift the icing sugar and flour into a bowl, and mix in the ground almonds. Lightly beat the egg whites with a fork, then fold them into the dry ingredients. Add the cooled, melted butter and lemon rind, and mix well.

Three-quarters fill each mould with the mixture and bake on the middle shelf of the oven for 10 minutes. Turn the tray around, and bake for another 5 to 10 minutes, until the tops are golden and spring back to the touch.

Leave in the tins for 5 minutes, then gently unmould onto a wire tray and leave to cool. Dust the friands with icing sugar to serve, or store them in an airtight container for up to 3 days.

MAKES 10

180 g butter (preferably
 unsalted)
200 g icing sugar
60 g plain flour, sifted
120 g ground almonds
5 large free-range egg whites
1 tsp grated lemon or
 orange rind
icing sugar for dusting

Anytime shortbread

Free shortbread from the restrictively narrow timeframe of Christmas, and make it throughout the year. Hallelujah.

Heat the oven to 150°C/Gas 2. Combine the butter, icing sugar and sea salt in a food processor and whiz until smooth.

Sift in the flour and rice flour, then pulse off and on, scraping down the sides from time to time, until the mixture gathers into a ball. Knead for a minute or two until smooth, then cut into two, wrap in cling film and refrigerate for 30 minutes.

Turn onto a floured surface and pat or lightly roll out the dough until 1 cm thick. Cut into 4 cm rounds, using a biscuit cutter or the rim of a liqueur glass. Reshape the scraps and cut more rounds. Place on a baking tray and prick with a fork.

Bake on the middle shelf of the oven for 10 minutes, then turn the tray around and bake for another 5 to 10 minutes until touched with colour. Leave to cool on the tray. Store the shortbread in an airtight container for up to 2 weeks.

MAKES 30
150g unsalted butter, soft
75g icing sugar
pinch of sea salt
150g plain flour
75g rice flour or cornflour

Coconut macaroons

You can't get much simpler than this: three little ingredients turned into crisp little coconut biscuits to serve with coffee, poached fruits, or the little lemon pots on page 160.

Heat the oven to 180°C/Gas 4. Whisk the egg whites, sugar and coconut together in a bowl until they lightly come together. With wet hands, press the mixture into a flat, square shape about 1cm high, on a board.

Cut out twelve 4 or 5cm rounds, using a small pastry cutter or upturned liqueur glass, and place on a lightly oiled or non-stick baking tray.

Bake in the centre of the oven for 15 minutes until very lightly golden, just touched with colour. Transfer the macaroons to a wire tray to cool. Store in an airtight container for up to 1 week.

MAKES 12
2 egg whites
100g caster sugar
160g desiccated coconut

just egg white, sugar and coconut

Espresso prunes

Dissolve 2 tbsp ground espresso coffee in 125 ml boiling water, then strain. Add 300 g sugar, 2 tbsp brandy and 500 ml water and bring to the boil, stirring. Add 500 g large dried, pitted prunes and gently simmer for 30 minutes until the liquid is thick and syrupy. Serve with yoghurt.

Chocolate bourbon balls

If you've ever made chocolate truffles, you will know they can be quite tricky. These aren't, but they are just as delicious. And if you're feeling flash, decorate with edible gold leaf, available from cake decoration shops.

Finely chop the chocolate. Heat the cream in a saucepan, stirring until it bubbles, then remove from the heat, add the chocolate and stir until melted.

Whiz the sponge fingers in a food processor, or crush with a rolling pin to fine crumbs.

MAKES 50

160g dark, bitter chocolate

125ml whipping cream

250g Italian sponge fingers (savoiardi)

100g icing sugar

3 tbsp cocoa powder

100g ground almonds

100g finely chopped walnuts

3 tbsp bourbon, or whisky

180g butter, melted

cocoa powder for dusting

Sift the icing sugar and cocoa powder into a large bowl. Mix in the crumbs, ground almonds and chopped walnuts. Add the bourbon, chocolate cream and butter and mix well.

Take a walnut-sized pinch of the mixture and roll into a ball in your hands. (If too wet, add a little more cocoa powder. If a little dry, add a dash more bourbon.) Place on greaseproof paper on a tray, and refrigerate for at least 4 hours until firm. Roll each chocolate bourbon ball in cocoa powder to serve.

recipe index

index

o

oats: Amish pancakes, 31
  oatcakes with goat cheese, 21
oil: sage-flavoured, 46
  spiced, 43
olives: French café salad, 57
  penne with tuna, 134
  Spanish meatballs, 61
  yellow pepper salad, 68
omelette, Asian, 143
onions, 108–11
  caramelised onions, 110
  chopping without tears, 110
  15 minute dinner, 111
  French onion soup, 110
  hash browns with bacon rolls, 148
  lamb steak sandwich, 53
  onion rings, 111
  onion sauce, 111
  onions with cheese, 146
  onions with tomatoes and sausages, 110
  roast onions, 111
  sweet and sour onions, 111
  sweet onion crostini, 28
orange flower water: Moroccan rice pud, 169
oranges: blood orange jelly, 164
  chilli orange duck, 114
  fruity drink, 40
orecchiette with rocket, 135
oysters, chipolata, 13

p

pancakes, Amish, 31
pancetta chicken, 115
parmesan lamb cutlets, 64
parsley: gremolata, 47
  parsley and lemon salad, 79
parsnips: roast tamari veg, 130
pasta: baked spaghetti, 137
  hot and cold tomato sauce for pasta, 87
  orecchiette with rocket, 135
pâtés: country terrine, 37
peaches: little peach tarts, 166
  roast vanilla peaches, 165

peanuts: caramel salmon and lime, 102
peeling tomatoes, 86
penne with tuna, 134
peppers: Asian duck salad, 83
  fattoush, 74
  gazpacho with cucumber, 20
  Tunisian salad rolls, 43
  warm Mediterranean veg, 50
  yellow pepper salad, 68
pesto: roast pesto chicken, 90
pies: chicken pies, 36
  little egg and ham pies, 33
pitta breads: fattoush, 74
  Tunisian salad rolls, 43
plums, sugar, 157
pork: Asian omelette, 143
  baked spaghetti, 137
  country terrine, 37
  pork with apple and sage, 92
potatoes: beef with shallots, 121
  blue cheese potato, 147
  crash hot potatoes, 99
  French café salad, 57
  hash browns with bacon rolls, 148
  penne with tuna, 134
  potato salad with gremolata, 47
  warm potatoes and capers, 71
prawns: coconut prawns with chilli, 23
prosciutto: Amish pancakes, 31
  figs and baked ricotta, 38
  sweet onion crostini, 28
prunes, espresso, 184
pulao, 153
pumpkin: roast tamari veg, 130

q

quail, honey soy, 63
quail eggs, spiced, 15

r

radishes: fattoush, 74
red-cooking, 153
relishes: easy tomato jam, 87
rhubarb sponge pud, 156

rice: beetroot rice, 101
  cinnamon coconut rice, 152
  Moroccan rice pud, 169
  pulao, 153
ricotta: figs and baked ricotta, 38
rocket: chorizo and sweet potato, 72
  crumbed goat cheese salad, 17
  French café salad, 57
  lamb steak sandwich, 53
  orecchiette with rocket, 135
  penne with tuna, 134

s

sage: fried sage leaves, 46
  pork with apple and sage, 92
salads, 67–83
  Asian duck salad, 83
  chicken Caesar, 80
  chorizo and sweet potato, 72
  crumbed goat cheese salad, 17
  fattoush, 74
  French café salad, 57
  grilled courgette salad, 69
  herby salads, 46
  parsley and lemon salad, 79
  potato salad with gremolata, 47
  sesame mangetout, 78
  Tunisian salad rolls, 43
  warm potatoes and capers, 71
  yellow pepper salad, 68
salmon: caramel salmon and lime, 102
  salmon in cabbage, 122
  teriyaki salmon, 125
salmoriglio dressing, 126
sandwiches: fresh herb sandwich, 46
  lamb steak sandwich, 53
sauces: hot and cold tomato sauce for pasta, 87
  instant tomato sauce, 86
  onion sauce, 111
  sticky cardamom toffee syrup, 152
  teriyaki, 125